UNTAMED
MUSHROOMS

UNTAMED MUSHROOMS

From Field to Table

A Midwestern Guide

Michael Karns

Dennis Becker

Lisa Golden Schroeder

MINNESOTA HISTORICAL SOCIETY PRESS

"Introduction," "Getting Started," "Tools and Tips," and "The Mushrooms" by Michael Karns. Creative direction and all photography by Dennis Becker. "A Time and Place" and "A Kitchen Handbook" with recipes and food styling for the photography by Lisa Golden Schroeder. Text, cover design, and illustrations by David Spohn.

www.mnhspress.org

The Minnesota Historical Society Press is a member of the Association of University Presses.

Manufactured in the United States of America

10 9 8 7 6 5 4 3 2 1

♾ The paper used in this publication meets the minimum requirements of the American National Standard for Information Sciences—Permanence for Printed Library Materials, ANSI Z39.48–1984.

International Standard Book Number
ISBN: 978-1-68134-086-9 (paper)

Library of Congress Cataloging-in-Publication Data

Names: Karns, Michael, author. | Becker, Dennis (Photographer), author. | Schroeder, Lisa Golden, author.
Title: Untamed mushrooms : from field to table / Michael Karns, Dennis Becker, Lisa Golden Schroeder.
Description: St. Paul, MN : Minnesota Historical Society Press, [2018] | Includes index.
Identifiers: LCCN 2017053889 | ISBN 9781681340869 (pbk. : alk. paper)
Subjects: LCSH: Cooking (Mushrooms) | Edible mushrooms.
Classification: LCC TX804 .K37 2018 | DDC 641.6/374—dc23
LC record available at https://lccn.loc.gov/2017053889

For my fungal friends and family far and wide. M.K.
For Kandace, Nick, and Joseph. D.B.
For Mark, Luke, Sam, and Jack—always. L.G.S.

And to Maizee, the studio dog who always greets us with a happy tail wag
and cleans up the little messes.

Contents

· · · · ·

Preface

When Dennis Becker and I started our blog, 2fish1dish.com, we set out to explore food or agricultural topics close to where we live. We wanted to learn about things we knew nothing about, and we wanted to feature everyday people doing interesting—and in some cases extraordinary—things, out of the limelight. We work in the commercial food world, so our creative energies needed stretching—and the beauty of the internet is we could fashion our storytelling in any way that pleased us. We've been fortunate to have an audience that likes the same things we do.

After learning about how to keep bees and make maple syrup, we set our sights on unraveling the mysteries of intentionally stumbling upon wild mushrooms. After a few leads to local foragers fell through, a colleague mentioned—with a raised eyebrow of surprise that we didn't already know—that someone else we worked with was The Mushroom Guy we needed to talk to. And it was Cowboy, a tall, somewhat taciturn digital technology expert I'd see on jobs. The guy who always wore a cowboy hat and pretty much kept to himself. In fact, I'd never talked to him, and I was a little bit afraid to approach him about whether he'd share a fraction of what he knew (come to find out he's a certified mushroom forager) with us. Mushroom hunters—even very amateur ones—are notoriously secretive. But I tracked him down, and lo and behold, he was actually friendly. And he was more than happy to take us out, tactically scouting favorite spots beforehand. As we trekked through the woods, it was sort of like going to Disneyland—every place he led us there was a cluster of a new and different species of incredible fungus, showing off for our benefit. Ours was a completely different experience than that of most people, who trudge along trails and up hills or rummage about in the woods for hours and hours—and never find a thing (or any edible thing, anyway). It was truly thrilling to see such extraordinary fruits of the earth, hiding out under fallen leaves or climbing high in the most dramatic way on towering trees. Dennis photographed and I recorded reams of storytelling and observations about what we saw and what

Michael shared. (I've never felt comfortable with nicknames unless I'm in on the naming, so Cowboy transformed into Michael—or The Professor in my mind.) We posted a long story about him and stalking wild mushrooms, complete with some entertaining video.

So now here we are, rounding up a more useful collection of intelligence to get you started, with the hope some of it will linger in your head as you begin to haunt your own local parks or forests or even your yard. And with the assumption that you are going to be successful—at least every once in a while—you can browse through our ideas for savoring your hard-gotten gains.

Lisa Golden Schroeder

· · · · ·

What do you think of when you hear the word *mushroom*? Do you think *'shrooms, man*, and picture a long-haired, tie-dyed, stoner type? Perhaps, if you're of a certain age, you visualize Mario becoming Super Mario or gaining Heart Points after capturing a mushroom or, conversely, if you're of another age, you may think of shearing your Mooshrooms in Minecraft and converting them into mushrooms and a cow in the electronic interface of the gaming world. Do you think of delicious things to eat, or are you more inclined to think *toadstool: gross!* You may carry a dread and fear of mushrooms from old wives' tales and folk mythologies. Regardless of your current feelings toward mushrooms, it is our intention, and indeed hope, to coax you into the fraternity of fungus-loving foragers.

This project grew out of Dennis and Lisa's blog, 2fish1dish.com. For their post "Stalking Mushrooms," they tagged along with me and my mushroom foraging friends to see what our infatuation is all about. That successful excursion planted just the right seed to grow into the most amazing collaboration. Lisa's experience with food of all manner, Dennis's fastidious attention to imagery, and my knowledge of the fungal world has coalesced into a publication that truly makes me proud to have had the opportunity to work with these amazing artists.

Contributors to the North American Mycoflora Project sort the continent's mycological taxonomy, an enormous task that is challenging, complex, and tedious. The time I dedicate to the project is my way of giving back to the fungal community and to our ecosystem at large. My enthusiasm for obsession means this kind of focused effort is right up my alley.

In my own work as a forager for foundfoods.com, I also offer the midwestern community a path to experience the delights of products that many people the world over would have commonly learned about growing up. With a focus on the fungal, I feel blessed beyond comprehension to do something I love every day.

Michael Karns

A Time and Place

A Mushrooming Affair

Local. No word better describes how we live. Community is local. Politics are local. And access to food is mostly local, though not as much as it once was. As I've worked on new ways to cook with our wild harvests, I've dipped in and out of discovering both Native and immigrant influences in our region, finding the obvious rewriting of traditional narratives. Ethnomycology—the study of how people use fungi—has a long and fascinating history.

The term *terroir* has classically been used to describe the character of wine grapes—the combination of soil, climate, and sunlight that creates distinctive character and expresses a sense of place that's defined by flavor. But it's also used to define the environmental factors, including relationships to other plants (especially trees), that set the stage for the quiet world of mushrooms to flourish. I think the term can describe people, too: we flourish depending on where we live, based on what's at hand. Getting out in the woods and fields to find food is a human endeavor, the hunting and gathering part of our history before we began to cultivate crops and domesticate animals. Hiding and seeking—not just a children's game, but a way to survive.

Indigenous peoples in the Midwest are the source of the first truly local cuisine with wild foods at its heart, but as the historical timeline advanced, people from all over the world made their way here. Our region is especially influenced by influxes of northern and eastern European immigrants, and in the more recent past refugees from southeastern Asia and Latin America. I listened to evocative stories from midwesterners whose families braved arduous travels to settle here, fortified by their hope for better lives. Norway, Sweden, Finland, Germany, Poland, Czechoslovakia, Thailand, Laos, and Mexico are just a handful of former homelands—and all share treasured family traditions, spanning several generations, of gathering wild mushrooms as the earth warms and cools over the seasons.

· · · · ·

Hope Flanagan is an early childhood educator at Minneapolis's Little Earth Neighborhood Learning Center's Native language immersion program—and also a respected Native storyteller. Born on a Seneca Indian reservation in upstate New York, she moved to Wisconsin as a small child and grew up immersed in Ojibwe culture, developing fluency in the language and traditions. Hope describes learning about wild foods and how the gathering of mushrooms was limited: they are valued more for their healing properties than as a food source. She told me that wild fungi are generally associated with death, as demonstrated in the Ojibwe language when referring to specific mushrooms. She did share stories of an Ojibwe elder who lives on Rainy Lake, which straddles the US border with Canada, and who harvests what she believes are king boletes and possibly *Lactarius* mushrooms. Hope hunts for morels in the spring—but finds that few of her friends are interested in eating them. She told of a much stronger tradition of gathering a wild lichen called rock tripe that grows from rocks and is highly nutritious. Long, wild stories revolving around this lichen exist within the Ojibwe, Dakota, and Ho-Chunk cultures, while mushrooms occupy a firm place in the tribal medicine chest.

John and Jola Rajtar embrace their Polish heritage and deeply rooted passion for wild mushrooms as part of the rhythm of each year. John is a good Minnesota boy, one of eight children, the son of Poles displaced by World War II. Like many second-generation kids with nostalgic parents from someplace else, he grew up with one foot in America and one foot in the Old World. Mushrooming plays a huge part in the culture and cuisine of Poland, and John and his wife, Jola, a native Pole, still hunt a wide variety of wild mushrooms that they dry and pickle for the winter months.

John's wistful remembrances of childhood autumns are filled with early-morning drives to secret places. Long sleeves, long pants, ticks, poison ivy . . . cold and wet. But also toting wooden-slatted apple bushel baskets, filling them up as his family fanned out across the forest floor, discovering the prizes hidden within the smell of earthiness and decay. He recalls spreading out newspaper and cleaning, trimming, and rinsing the mushrooms. They would be dried or marinated, preserved in myriad ways because it was essential to have mushrooms for the all-important holiday recipes: Christmas *barszcz*, pierogi, and game stews. In a Polish household, that very specific, wild, wonderful flavor is the taste of traditional dishes.

John remembers a kitchen cupboard where a linen bag, filled with dried mushrooms sent (or smuggled) by family from Poland, was stored, along with long strands of dried mushrooms threaded onto strings. These days, John and Jola keep time-honored foodways alive, making mushroom pierogi (dumplings; see page 275) and bigos, a hunter's stew defined by the flavor of wild fungi.

A favorite is *borowiki*, or king boletes. Now Slavic flavors—fermented, foraged, whole-grain, and herbal—are having a renaissance.

Bᴇᴀ Kʀɪɴᴋᴇ was born in the Lüneburger Heide region of Germany, just south of Hamburg. She recalls her parents, who were of German ancestry but grew up in Estonia, taking her out mushroom picking when she was a small child. After World War II they emigrated to central Minnesota to raise the family on a farm and a shoestring, so Bea learned early about foraging and growing food. She's still an avid gardener and has faint memories of the "yellow champignons" her mother would stir into green split pea soup. She told me that mushrooming is terrifically popular in Estonia, perhaps because of its strong forest culture. She mentioned being struck, on a long-ago trip to the summer house of old family friends, by a kitchen shelf lined with jars of pickled mushrooms—and how it made her feel at home. A registered dietician and former instructor at the University of Minnesota's School of Public Health, she maintains a strong interest in the sociological roles of food in various cultures.

I met Mᴇᴀᴅᴏᴡ Aᴅᴀᴍs through her mother, Jᴜʟɪᴇ Kᴇᴀɴ. Living on the edge of the boundary waters of northern Minnesota, Julie combs the woods for birch bark and willow branches that she weaves into baskets for berry gathering and mushroom hunting, along with harvesting other wild plants. Meadow, an accomplished wilderness photographer, began hunting for wilderness edibles and medicinal plants as a young girl, taught by her mom. A few years ago, a friend from the Czech Republic introduced her to searching for golden chanterelles. Already quite familiar with morels, she became enamored of the brilliant beauty and flavor of chanterelles and is as passionate about the season as any longtime hunter. Her favorite way with them is in a quick butter sauté with chicken and garlic. But if she dries them, she likes to reconstitute them as a miso soup or cook them directly in a heartier brothy soup with ginger, garlic, onion, a little meat, venison or beef broth, and some dried seaweed (see page 292 for a mushroom dashi stock). At the peak of chanterelle season— usually in early to mid-August—she'll take off a couple days from work to get outside, her mind filled with dreams of overflowing baskets. Her thoughts echo ours: a walk in the woods is never a waste.

Yɪᴀ Vᴀɴɢ is a Hmong immigrant, born in Thailand. But he's also an American. Arriving in the States as a young child, he grew up in Lancaster County, Pennsylvania, and Manitowoc, Wisconsin. More comfortable holding a boning knife than a T-ball bat as a kid, on Saturday mornings he often headed to Amish farms to buy a whole hog with his family instead of playing ball. But as he got older he also loved American burgers. Now as a super-charged chef (or cook, the term he prefers), he's building new awareness around Hmong flavors that are firmly rooted in where he lives, still respecting his cultural past and family traditions but taking them on a test drive, exploring new boundaries and embracing the land he stands on now.

Given the huge Hmong community in the Upper Midwest, I was curious about his mushroom foraging experiences. Yia enthusiastically shared his point of view about food and cooking—and opened my eyes to some geopolitical and environmental truths. The Hmong people, who fled to the mountains during the political unrest of the 1960s and '70s in Southeast Asia, do have a strong foraging tradition. But according to Yia, it was for wild greens and other survivalist edibles, not for mushrooms we would recognize here. Traditional culinary use of mushrooms is prevalent in Hmong cooking, but it's more about rehydrating dried black fungus and other Asian mushrooms. He suggested that certain mushrooms that grow in Thailand and Laos were prized and eaten only by the more affluent, not the poorer refugees who became part of the world-wide diaspora during the years after the Vietnam War.

Once in America, Yia's father often jumped out of the car to gather wild watercress or other field greens he glimpsed from the window. Wild mushroom hunting was not on the radar. But that doesn't stop Yia. He welcomes wild mushrooms in the season (mostly acquired from local foragers), using authentic dishes as a diving platform to switch things up, swapping in meaty chicken of the woods or hen of the woods for the real thing—often surprising diners at his traveling pop-up restaurant events. Lemongrass, ginger, garlic, and chile-spiced mushrooms are heavily smoked and chopped, then tossed into large bowls of fried rice, fooling eaters into thinking that the smoky and richly-spiced mush-rooms are bits of beef or pork jerky.

Here's my own riff on an idea Yia shared—just one of many experiments with traditional and new ingredients, what he calls dorking around in the kitchen. "We came up with an umami bomb of a finishing salt; a good shake will even get dudes to eat vegetables," he told me with a grin.

hmong-inspired umami salt

makes about 1⅓ cups

1 cup Korean sea salt

2 tablespoons fish sauce

1½ teaspoons grated lime zest

⅓ cup crushed or pulverized dried lobster, king bolete, or blend of woodland mushrooms

crushed dried Thai (bird's eye or chile de árbol) chile or chiles pequeños to taste

Heat oven to 300 degrees. Mix the salt with the fish sauce and lime zest. Spread out the mixture onto a parchment-lined rimmed baking sheet. Place in oven; bake for about 20 minutes or until dried, flaky, and starting to brown around the edges. Rake the salt mixture with a fork to break up lumps. Mix in the dried mushrooms and chiles. Spoon into a jar or grinder bottles. Store in a cool, dark place for up to 2 months.

kitchen notes

Korean sea salt is also called brining salt; it's the stuff used to make fermented foods like kimchi. Minimally processed, the grains are larger and have a lower sodium content then other salts. Yia likes how large and flaky it is. Mixed with a good fish sauce (salted and fermented anchovies), then slowly dried in the oven, this umami salt boasts a seasoning quotient that is really boosted with the final addition of intensely flavored dried mushrooms and the heat of the chiles. Yia suggests sprinkling the salt blend over grilled parsnips or carrots; I love it tossed with roasted cauliflower.

Introduction

Awalk in the woods. What could be better? It can be carefree or meditative; it can be intentional and educational or even therapeutic. It can be many things all at once or an utterly singular consideration. A walk in the woods may be a foreign concept. The city dweller, confined in a concrete community, may find the woods a distant idea or a boring one; the more rural dweller may consider it mundane, unremarkable due to overexposure. But many people are reverent of the forest. They consider its canopy and its columns of ancient trunks to be hallowed halls—even, perhaps, a place of spiritual contemplation and sanctuary. We all have our reasons for taking a walk, but the purpose here is to collect fare for the table. Fungal fare, to be precise.

Mushrooms are truly enigmatic sources of sustenance and sublime flavor experiences. The history of eating wild mushrooms reaches so far into our past that we cannot accurately define when the practice of collecting them as a food began or even venture a guess as to whether we began consuming them as incidentals before we evolved as hominids. Dipping a toe into the vast pool that is the history and lore of wild mushrooms, a study known as ethnomycology, introduces one to a world as bizarre and mind-bending as any proffered by Alice and her trip down the rabbit hole. Every culture on the globe, save those confined to icy lands without the soil or host to support edible fungus, has some connection to mushrooms.

Any day I set out in search of wild mushrooms is ultimately a day I set out to simply walk in the woods. I never know if I will be successful in finding my intended bounty, but the fact is that the only way to know the woods and understand the cycles of fungal life in an area or to discover a new patch is to walk in the woods. While many environmental factors offer keys to considering a landscape's viability—soil moisture, tree species, shade/sun exposure—the simple fact is that mushrooms grow where they decide to grow, and developing known spots requires a commitment to really understanding a place. Some years, a spot will fruit in quantities that will truly challenge one's ability to pick them before they fade into the inevitable oblivion of mush. In other years, a spot might produce only a few specimens or not fruit at all.

One of the great challenges of the avid picker is hitting the right spots at the right time. This proposition becomes somewhat easier after years of scouting the same places, but one can also be quite surprised at unusual times, so it behooves the "expert" to check his or her patches often. Just a quick walk through an area known to produce black trumpets has yielded a full basket for me even at odd times of the season. Walking a favorite black morel patch out of season revealed one of my best *Gyroporus cyanescens* sources, which now annually produces a hearty basket full of these amazing, dynamic bluing boletes.

Rainfall is another important factor when considering what patches to explore in a given season. Often I will check the radar and soil moisture maps provided by agricultural extension offices, online resources that help me better understand where mushrooms may be more likely to fruit.

Seeking areas of mesic soil regimes (those with a balanced moisture supply) will improve success as these tracts are often better at producing bountiful fruitings. Rainfall is important in this aspect, but oftentimes even when rainfall is scarce, such as in late July and August, one can find low-lying areas that will yield large numbers of mushrooms. Hunting along streams or in low areas, as well as on the edges of the Midwest's many lakes, can be productive. On the shoreline road around one northern Minnesota lake, in a stretch about a mile and a half long, I regularly find ten or so large fruitings of chicken of the woods each year. This area is so consistent that it's almost impossible to make that drive between late July and the end of September and not see a gorgeous flush of chickens.

On cold winter days, my fitness tracker is an embarrassing reminder that I am not moving, much in contrast to the warmer months, when I hunt for my wild fungal prey. In winter, my numbers are in the three-thousand-steps range, but during peak morel season I might log twenty to thirty thousand steps in a day. One might balance the number of steps with the number of mushrooms, but the figures can be deceiving. Looking back on my logs and journal entries, the days with fifteen thousand steps tend to denote high success: fewer miles walked because so much time was spent harvesting. Foragers collect spots, or what we like to call "patches": places in a region where one can consistently expect to find a particular species of mushroom. In time one gathers a vast resource of patches to check, eventually leading to a library of foraging locations that increases one's return on invested time and allows greater success from season to season. My patches, discovered over many years of walking in fields and forests, range from thousand-plus acres of public land to backyard stumps of friends who have inquired about the "crazy" thing growing in their yard.

Many people are reticent to ask a stranger to allow them to walk on private land, but I have found farmers and rural landowners to be quite welcoming, especially when I offer to share my knowledge and bounty. I have spotted, from the highway at fifty miles per hour, chicken of the woods growing in someone's yard and turned around to knock on a door, explain my interest, and ask if I can harvest the alien-looking fungus—only to have the homeowner explain that there is a much larger flush of that "weird-looking stuff" in the woods behind the house and I am welcome to it all. Don't be shy, but always remember to ask permission. You do yourself, and other would-be foragers, a great disservice if you trespass.

I find that hunting for mushrooms, and foraging for wild edibles in general, is an endeavor as much about the pursuit as the goal. Even when my search results in few or no mushrooms, I may still consider my effort a great success. Many times I have found a new patch to revisit by spotting the remnants of an old specimen. Chicken of the woods is particularly good at leaving behind a trace of the old to give a clue for a spot to check in the future. Other times it's simply noticing an area of good habitat or an overlooked copse of dying elms. Many other edibles grow in the woods, from ramps to wild rhubarb, from blueberries to Labrador tea (*Rhododendron groenlandicum*). There is always something to make the walk worth the time; it may simply be the fresh air.

Minnesota is home to some of the most diverse forest types in the United States: the Laurentian Mixed Forest of the northeastern region; the Eastern Broadleaf Forest cutting a diagonal swath from the Mississippi River valley in the southeast to the headwaters at Itasca State Park; Aspen Parkland in the northwest corner; and Prairie Parkland ranging down the western side of the state and spreading across the southern region eastward to the I-35 corridor. This variety of forest type combined with a temperate climate facilitates the remarkable fungal assortment available here in Minnesota.

The kingdom of fungus is immense and expansive, second only to that of insects in breadth and scope, and far less understood. In this huge world of fungus, as within the plant world, only a relative few are edible—and fewer still are truly delectable.

One fortunate aspect of the foraging endeavor is the change of seasons and the accompanying shift in variety. While there are certainly some overlaps in varietal availability throughout the growing season, there is often a distinct changing of the guard. In spring, the beginning of the season is announced by the greatly celebrated morels and the common pheasant back. As spring gives way to summer, rivers of golden chanterelles run bountiful through the forests. Lobsters and chickens proliferate as summer heats up and the days reach their

longest. Finally come the black trumpets, lion's mane, shaggy manes, the fall favorite hen of the woods, and, of course, the king boletes.

While we cover a solid baker's dozen fungus species in this treatise, several are part of a historical grouping known as the "foolproof four," originally presented in Clyde M. Christensen's book *Common Edible Mushrooms*, published by the University of Minnesota Press in 1943. Morels, golden chanterelles, chicken of the woods, and giant puff-balls—these mushrooms are generally considered to be safe to eat for most people, are easily identified, and have no deadly look-alikes.

Many people equate mushrooms of any kind with the black, slug-like, slimy or mostly flavorless spongy bits in their food. Midwestern-ers are probably more often exposed to the canned variety ubiquitous in our region's official fare, "hot dish." Whatever the favorite hot dish version, it's sure to include a can of cream of mushroom soup. This is about as adventurous as the average person gets where mushrooms are concerned. Yes, there are the occasional brushes with the exotic in Asian cuisine or the odd exposure to an unusual variety at the whim of a restauranteur, but Americans are, by many measures, mushroom avoidant.

Around the globe are cultures that cherish the world of fungus. In these places, mushrooms are as much a part of a culture's cuisine as any vegetable or meat. Markets in France, Italy, Spain, or the central European countries display enormous baskets of dozens of mushroom varieties. In Asian cultures some varietals, considered medicinal, have been revered for centuries. The Lingzhi, a species of *Ganoderma*, has been virtually worshipped for more than two thousand years. Eastern Europeans hold all edible mushrooms in very high regard, and they will go an extra mile to make a perfectly questionable variety passably palatable. This treatment may involve boiling the mushrooms mul-tiple times and casting off the water before pickling or brining. This effort—and its result—do not inspire me to collect the many species that my Polish-Czech grandmother or her ancestors might have. These practices, though persistent in many cultures, were most likely born of scarcity rather than veneration. In the United States, appreciation for wild mushrooms is increasing, and some varietals are now cultivated for market. The shiitake mushroom, an Asian species which has become almost synonymous with the term *wild mushroom* in US restaurants, is in fact a cultivated fungus that has seen a marked increase in sales over the past decade.

When I open a menu at a nice restaurant and find the words "wild mushrooms," I ask my server to inquire with the chef as to which

variety of wild mushrooms they're serving. Nine times out of ten I am told the selection includes maitake, shiitake, crimini, portobello, and sometimes even an admission of "button" mushrooms—NONE of which are "wild" and the last three of which are the same species differentiated only by age and growing process. You read that right, folks: the common button, portobello, and crimini mushrooms are all *Agaricus bisporus*. A matured common white button mushroom exposed to some daylight results in a portobello, and crimini are simply a brown variety of the same species.

Why does this bother me? Well, the real sticking point is that a cultivated hen of the woods, though generally very consistent in taste compared to other cultivated hens, does not taste like a wild hen. Perhaps it is the sugars or other compounds that wild mushrooms obtain in subterranean negotiations with their mycorrhizal partners or the saprobic sampling from so many differing hosts, but every wild mushroom I've harvested has had a unique, if only subtly different, flavor from its cultivated counterpart.

I've also noticed a distinct difference in the flavor quality between chanterelles sourced from the Pacific Northwest and those I've harvested myself in the Midwest. I believe the chanterelles found in Minnesota, while smaller and unquestionably less prolific, have a better flavor than the variety found out west. Don't get me wrong: I am a great fan of cultivated mushrooms, even the lowly button mushroom. Many grocers now carry some variety of mushroom species that can be persuaded to fruit in controlled conditions, and a few stores have quite the assortment. During the harvest season, local farmers' markets are an option for some people to find wild foraged mushrooms in their communities.

Finally, it's a principle thing. Don't tell me you're serving me a wild mushroom when in fact it was grown in a stainless-steel and glass laboratory for fungus. When I see the words "wild mushrooms," I like to imagine that I'm being offered a mushroom that was collected by a forager, a mushroom that doesn't take to cultivation, a mushroom that I can't go buy at my local supermarket—a mushroom that has a little bit of rogue that won't be tamed.

Getting Started

Some Rules for Mushroom Foraging

When in doubt, throw it out. Period. NEVER take a chance with a mushroom species if you are not one hundred percent confident of its identification. There is no culinary experience worth risking your health, let alone your life. Experimentation is not an option with regard to uncertain mushroom species.

Never trespass. Just don't do it. If you can't find the landowner, leave those mushrooms to spread their spores. This goes for private land as well as lands that are protected by federal, state, and county agencies. Many county lands have very strict rules regarding collection of ANY resource. For example, staff of the suburban Twin Cities Three Rivers Parks are especially aggressive in policing and controlling access to land in their parks. One can incur harsh fines for "leaving the trail" or for collecting ANY resource, including berries and mushrooms. Such collecting is allowed in state parks and generally not considered a threat to the health of the host or the ecosystem; it's a perfectly safe and sound use of public land. Still, it's important to know the rules.

It is not difficult to ask permission, and in most instances where I have asked to forage on a stranger's land I have been welcomed. Practice your social skills: they'll come in handy in other pursuits as well.

Tread lightly. Certain cultures maintain a deep connection to foraging for food, but in my travels I've noticed that some cultures have less respect for stewardship of wild resources. I have happened upon other foragers in state parks and protected forests who were collecting botanical species, an activity that carries quite a hefty fine and shows a great disrespect for our parks and the conservation personnel who protect these lands.

I have also walked through state park woods that look as if a division of infantry had gone before me: all the vegetation trampled flat and every mushroom

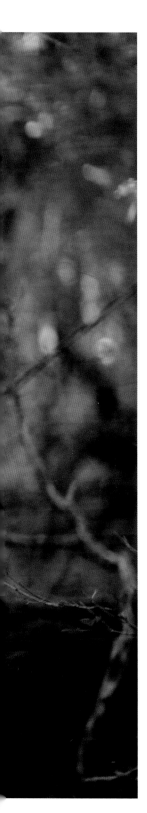

cut, with old or unwanted specimens toppled, crushed, or cast aside. The ground looked stunned and broken. No single culture or group is responsible for this kind of offense, but it remains our duty to protect wild lands and the resources they provide and to inform and educate those we meet along the way. Take great care to avoid destroying habitat or tramping upon the ground cover that provides shade and protects our mushroom pickings from pounding rain.

Stay on trail as much as possible when you're in parks, and tread carefully when you venture off-trail. Bushwhacking through the under-brush, I have had many close calls with ground nesting birds and even young fawns. Look before you step. A fawn will instinctively flatten itself on the ground and will not move even if you tread right next to it; naturally camouflaged as they are, it would be quite easy to step on one.

Don't pick mushrooms just because they're there. If you're not going to collect it for identification purposes or to eat it, leave it unmolested. Mushrooms, like all other organisms of forest and field, serve a purpose: let them stand if you won't be using them. Never dig or rake the soil or leaf litter in search of mushrooms. It is important to protect the myce-lium (the rooting, or vegetative part of the fungus, which reaches like branches underground or through decaying wood or leaves), so forage responsibly and carefully.

Never collect mushrooms from a questionable environment.

Mushroom mycelia are bioremediators, meaning they can remove toxic elements from the soil and sometimes concentrate those toxins within the fruiting bodies of the mushroom. Collecting mushrooms from areas that are regularly sprayed with hazardous chemicals could pose a great risk to your health. Apple orchards were once sprayed with lead arsenate pesticides; harvesting mushrooms in these landscapes could potentially result in arsenic and/or lead poisoning. Other areas to avoid are railroad beds, powerline rights of way, cemeteries, golf courses, and municipal parks where herbicides and pesticides are commonly used. Many park trails host a bounty of mushrooms but are sprayed regularly to control poison ivy, buckthorn, or other unwanted plants. Picking along such paths is discouraged. Ask park personnel about use of chemicals.

Separate mushrooms by species in the field and in the kitchen.

At least in the beginning it is a good idea to divide collected specimens by type as you learn to identify them. I use small waxed-paper bags to keep unusual finds or collection specimens separate from normal table fare varieties in the field. This process helps ensure that unknown species don't end up in the pot or on your plate. Take notes on where new oddities are found: what kind of soil, how heavy the forest canopy was, how much light, what species of trees and plants it might be associated with—all this information will be helpful in identifying a mushroom.

Buy a field guide or identification resource. Buy two or three. One thing is certain: if you become a full-fledged mycophile, you're going to need resources, and no single book does it all. Also, just roll up your sleeves and get comfortable with the Latin. The common names for mushrooms are slippery, changing from region to region. Learning the Latin, even if names shift over time due to further scientific study, is far less painful than you might expect. Regardless of potential changes, the historical name will still be relevant.

David Arora's *Mushrooms Demystified* is the standout print resource for the serious mushroom forager. It has great keys, and Arora's writing is straightforward and does not bog down in the minutia of mycological science. Books by Michael Kuo, *100 Edible Mushrooms* and, with Andrew S. Methven, *Mushrooms of the Midwest*, are both fantastic resources, and Kuo's www.mushroomexpert.com web resource is an unparalleled and remarkable collection of mycological data. Kuo's writing is humorous and lighthearted yet pertinent and informative.

Identifying Mushrooms

First, a caveat: this book is intended in NO way to be an identification guide. Far more qualified folks have dedicated their entire lives to mycology and the production of such resources. Instead, we aim to provide an approachable discussion of techniques involved in using the edible mushrooms you collect. In my exploration of the mushroom kingdom, certain strategies have benefited my study more than others and made the whole 'ology part of mycology less academic and more interesting. Here's an outline of my process for taking a new species of suspected edible from field to table.

When I come upon an unknown mushroom and wish to determine its species, I first make some notes about where and when I found it. Not simply the region of the state, but the actual forest or field type. How much light is getting to the mushroom? I write down the plant species in the vicinity I can identify. Is there water nearby? Am I at the top, middle, or bottom of a hill or ridge? Does the landscape orient to a cardinal direction? In other words, if the mushroom is growing on a slope, does the site face north, south, east, or west? Is it growing in dirt or on wood or possibly buried wood or a root? Be very clear about this.

An example is instructive. Sometimes a mushroom will grow in soil collected in a decaying log. When educating people on mushrooms, I show photographs of a beautiful destroying angel (*Amanita bisporigera*) growing from a dead log. A novice could easily make the mistake that this deadly poisonous mushroom that grows in soil and is mycorrhizal with certain trees appears to be growing from wood. Upon closer examination, one can see that there is just enough soil collected in the crevice and the wood has decayed enough that this ground dweller successfully sprouted in an unusual spot.

What other characteristics might be pertinent? Is there a heavy leaf layer or pine needles on the ground? Is the soil sandy or dark and rich or hard-packed and more claylike? Is the soil dry or wet? All these notations will help you with future observations and will, ideally, prevent the frustration of having to throw out an unidentified mushroom.

Next, I collect and individually bag several specimens. If possible, take multiple mushrooms at differing stages of development. When collecting for identification, do not cut your specimens; instead, dig out the base of the mushroom as well. Certain species have telltale characteristics revealed only by excavation, such as a long taproot or a cup-shaped volva or even sprouting from an insect larva. Be delicate and deliberate to ensure that your samples get home in one piece.

Once you have your prizes back where you can study them, photograph the specimens from several angles, being sure to document each stage of growth in your other samples as well. Take photos of the whole mushrooms, then of the top and bottom of caps, if present. Next, photograph the flesh of the cap after breaking off a piece to note any staining or color change in the flesh. Repeat this process with the stem. Break or cut the stem lengthwise, taking note of the interior structure, and record any color changes or bruising of the flesh inside or out. Pay close attention to the base of the stem when cutting this cross section. Some stem bases will change color when cut or broken.

Take note of other characteristics. What do your specimens smell like? Is it a pleasant odor? Some mushrooms have a very potent and offensive chemical or creosote smell, while others smell of black licorice or watermelon rind. The terminology involved in identifying mushroom odors can be disconcerting and even bewildering if one delves deeply enough into the literature to brush up against such descriptors as *farinaceous* or *phenolic* or (and no, I'm not kidding) *spermatic*, but worry not. Just make your notes and remember that everyone smells things somewhat differently, just as we each see color a bit differently, and some people can smell certain odors and not others. Smell is just another clue in our bag of tricks.

Mushrooms can be tasted, but I recommend this approach only to those who are familiar enough with the deadly poisonous mushrooms to ensure that

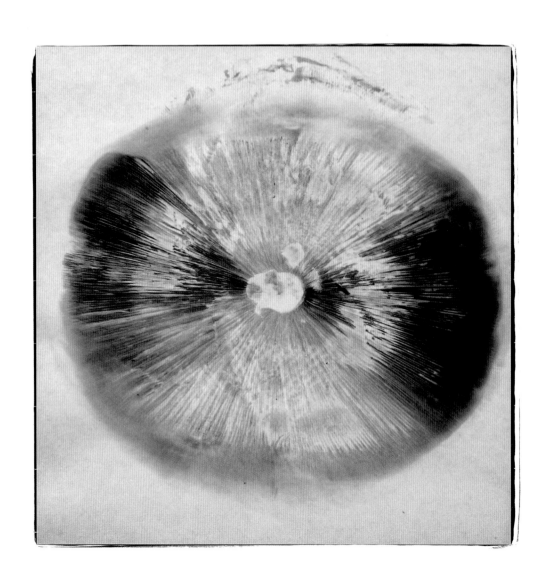

they are not taste-testing a killer. Never put a deadly mushroom variety in your mouth. Period.

If you are comfortable that the mushroom you're studying is not of the lethal variety, pinch off a small piece of the cap, ideally with some gill or tube material, about the size of a raisin, roll it on the tip of your tongue for a moment, and spit it out. Wait just about a minute. Now rinse out your mouth. What did it taste like? Is the taste mild or strong? Does it have a peppery hotness or a bitterness to it? Does it taste mild and/or pleasant? Make thorough notes on these aspects, and carry on.

Next, it's time for art class. You need to make a spore print. Spore color is a significant clue in determining a mushroom's identity. Some people use paper, white or black or sometimes both by laying a piece of black paper slightly overlapping a piece of white and placing the cap of the mushroom with the stem removed gill-side down on top of the overlap. Thus, one gets a visible spore print regardless of whether the spores are light or dark in color. I prefer a piece of glass or clear plexiglass: the transparent substrate allows me to place it on a dark or light background and still maintain the integrity of the overall print. One can also use a piece of aluminum foil, on which both light and dark spore prints will show up well. I like to photograph the spore print, too, and add the images to my collection data.

While these techniques may seem like overkill, they will serve you well if you happen to fall in love with mushroom foraging. The edible mushrooms featured in this book do not require this kind of vetting, but good habits are worth developing if you find yourself delving into trickier species.

From this point, it is a matter of following a good identification key such as those in David Arora's *Mushrooms Demystified* to tease out the results. With a little experience, this process becomes quicker, but with all the differing varieties of fungus out there it is rarely easy, and sometimes it is simply impossible without microscopic and chemical study. If you find all this effort overwhelming, remember that when the foraging season is over you'll have countless hours of free time, and with all this data you can armchair mushroom hunt through the worst of what a midwestern winter may bring.

Tools and Tips

What to Carry, What to Wear

Knives and Brushes. Whether you're apt to pinch off a mushroom at its base or cut it, a knife is a necessity in the field. Even though chanterelles are easily plucked and kings topple clean over with a nudge, some fungus, such as chicken of the woods or pheasant back, are better harvested with a blade. For most foraging, I'm partial to a folding knife: just a medium-sized blade that fits nicely in your hand. I also keep a fillet knife in my backpack for harvesting hen of the woods. The long, thin blade makes reaching up under a large hen much easier and allows me to collect these sometimes colossal fungus without tearing out the mycelial root.

I like a pair of shears or garden pruners when harvesting black trumpets. The shears cut cleanly without pulling up dirt and debris, and I can cut a handful at a time—a big help when faced with an epic day of picking. In the past when I harvested only with a knife I would sometimes arrive home after a long day of foraging mushrooms with a groove cut into my thumb from pinching the soft, tender stems between my knife blade and thumb. This could develop into a painful problem over the course of multiple foraging days in a row. Shears are not without their risks: I have also snipped my finger when cutting clumps of black trumpets. Caution and attention are wise when wielding any edged tool.

Even if you pick instead of cut your mushrooms, it's best to trim the stems before placing them in your basket or bag. The least amount of dirt deposited with your mushrooms the better. Cleaning wild mushrooms can be a chore, and it's best to minimize the task in every way possible. Trimming your picks and brushing away soil, leaf litter, and other debris as you go will make your kitchen work far more pleasant. I always keep several brushes in my kit and wear a special MushBrush on a lanyard around my neck.

NEVER put a dirty mushroom in your bag or basket. It's far easier to remove the dirt and debris while picking than to try to tease it out from between the folds and nooks and crannies of gills and teeth after your mushrooms have bounced around in a basket all day.

Baskets and Bags. I prefer to use a basket or a bucket, particularly five-gallon buckets drilled with several hundred quarter-inch holes. These work very well for most collecting and are especially great for black trumpets.

My mushroom bucket is outfitted with a tool holster mounted to the outside; the holster has dedicated slots for a fixed-blade knife, a few extra brushes, and a pair of heavy-duty kitchen shears or gardening pruners. I found a plastic kitchen storage container that fits into the top of the bucket with its lip overhanging slightly to hold it up like a deeply indented lid. This configuration serves several functions. First, it acts as a lid, keeping sticks, leaves, and insects from falling into the main section. Next, it helps in redistributing the mushrooms, especially if I'm picking a delicate species like trumpets and happen upon a heftier variety such as hedgehogs or a fat king bolete. I can continue to pick, tossing them all together in the top, and when it gets full I can transfer the lighter variety to the bottom section and carry on. A final benefit is that, with the bowl-in-a-bucket system, the bowl also has a lid: in the event of a rain shower, placing the lid on the bowl in the top of your bucket keeps your whole harvest relatively dry.

A woven basket is another great option for carrying mushrooms. I have several willow foraging baskets made by an artisan in Britain, superbly fitted to the task of cradling my collections. In truth, any basket is better suited to success than a plastic shopping bag you found in your trunk. A fairly shallow basket about five inches deep and narrow rather than wide with a short handle is ideal for maneuvering through bushes. The minimal depth keeps the mushrooms on the top from getting too heavy for those on the bottom. Try not to overcrowd your basket. Piling some mushrooms too high will produce more mush than mushrooms at the end of the day. Giving your mushrooms some space and not smothering them will ensure that your dishes are prepared with the best specimens.

Folks often ask about using mesh bags that may help distribute mushroom spores. Let me be clear: it is very unlikely that you are benefiting the mushroom ecology in ANY way by collecting and carrying your mushrooms in a mesh bag. Mushroom spores are unlikely to fall from your bag and take up root as you travel along in your foraging. The air around us is laden with tens of thousands of spores; we inhale several spores with each and every breath. It is very rare, thankfully so,

that mushroom spores successfully take hold in the soil or a bark crevice and grow into the mycelial body necessary to bear fruit. If the process were not so complex and rare a thing, we would surely be completely blanketed in mycelia. While you are likely not helping the mushroom ecology by carrying your mushrooms in mesh bags, you are not harming it either, but you are most certainly shredding delicate morels and crushing chanterelles and trumpets as you stuff them into your bags. Mesh bags are ill-suited for harvesting most mushrooms, but chickens and lobsters seem to fare better in them than others.

Electronic Technology. One of the most indispensable items I carry into the woods with me is my cell phone. I know, I know: after all my talk about the woods being a sanctuary and a place of spiritual connection, why would I suggest bringing the cursed cell phone along? Well, there are several reasons. First, in many of the places where I forage, I do still get cell reception, so on the off chance something came up, like a twisted ankle or a broken bone, I would be able to reach out for help.

The woods can be a dangerous place, and when foraging it's important to keep an eye out for potential hazards. Ground-nesting yellow jackets can be quite aggressive when they have determined that you're an unwanted party near their home. (We had quite an unforgettable experience with them while foraging for this book.) And don't forget to look up: yellow jackets and bald-faced hornets make paper nests in trees as well. I have found them anywhere from one foot to thirty or forty feet off the ground, so keep this in mind while pushing through the underbrush. Making a mad dash through the forest while being swarmed by angry stingers is a good way to get that broken bone I mentioned earlier.

All of this is to say that it never hurts to have a connection to the world if an emergency arises. But the biggest reason for carrying my phone is to use it as a photo diary. I constantly document the many fungal features I find, providing a remarkable resource for remembering where and when I saw a particular mushroom and also reference to the date when unusual mushrooms were found. I always photograph my haul at the end of each foraging day as well so I have a record of when my best edibles fruited. As a supplement to my written journal of observations, the photos give me a great tool to better predict foraging success in the future.

Lastly, I keep the Audubon Mushrooms Mobile Field Guide app on my phone for when I need to look up a detail about an oddity discovered along the way.

I do suggest putting your phone on silent and turning off your notifications to make your experience in the outdoors much richer and more rewarding.

Clothing. In foraging fashion, function wins out over form. I prefer long pants and a long-sleeved shirt even when picking lobster mushrooms on a ninety-five-degree day with ninety percent humidity. Perhaps you question my sensibility if not my sanity. However, the function of this habit is worth the discomfort. I find it far less bothersome to sweat for a bit than to come home scratched, stabbed, and abraded from rock and thorn or, worse, covered in poison ivy or cow parsnip. Once you've had a shower following such a sweaty day, the suffering seems more a badge of honor and the remains end up down the drain, forgotten.

I prefer a heavy pant such as Carhartt or even a waxed cotton field pant like Filson's shelter brush pants. I turn to lightweight hiking pants only when summer heat and humidity peaks. I never resort to shorts. Heavy fabrics will protect against most thorns, though prickly ash will still get through my Carhartts. Only my Filson field pants or chaps are a match for the prickly ash, and they are utterly impervious to stinging nettles. An added benefit of the Filson shelter brush pants is that in the late summer through fall hitchhiking plants like burdock, horehound, cocklebur, and stick-tights don't easily attach to the waxed cotton fabric.

An example of choosing form over function: a friend joined me on an autumn foray dressed in those comfortable athletic fabric pants typically selected for lounging at home. By the end of the day those pants had to be thrown away because there was simply no hope of removing the thousands of attached burrs burrowed deeply into the fabric. I suggested he should just bury them and let the plants enjoy their success. They had obviously won the day.

Aside from the protection long pants and sleeves offer from prickers, they also act as a barrier to bugs. Mosquitos can be utterly insufferable in some areas where mushrooms love to grow, and the very serious threat of tick-borne diseases only adds to the list of benefits of proper dress. Beyond these points I have one other hard-and-fast rule where dress is concerned, and it has nothing to do with fashion. The fashion is up to you. Make a statement; go crazy. Wear stripes and plaids together. Tuck your pant legs into your socks. But whatever else you do, make sure that all your outer clothing including your socks and boots are treated against ticks.

My preferred clothing treatment is Permethrin, which lasts through several washings. It is a bit more of a hassle to use than DEET, as it requires treating your clothes prior to use and letting them dry. However, in my experience it is unquestionably more effective. I can always tell if

I've let an article of clothing go too long between treatments as I will inevitably find a bloodsucking hitchhiker on that item. Permethrin is incredibly effective in repelling ticks. It seems to be somewhat less effective on mosquitos than twenty-five-percent DEET products, but it is still a good deterrent.

DEET is also troublesome because it coats your clothing and rubs off on your hands, where it can transfer easily to your mushrooms. DEET is not safe to consume, and since we can't wash our mushrooms well enough to remove it, we must be cautious with how we use it while harvesting. While Permethrin is wet, it should be handled with great caution. But once Permethrin has dried on clothing, it is completely inert and safe, and rewetting the clothing does not reactivate the toxicity. Never spray Permethrin on clothes while you are wearing them.

Treating your clothes may seem unnecessary, but I implore you to guard against a potential tick-borne disease in any way you can. There are more than ten such ailments in the United States ranging from viruses to parasites, some of which can be deadly, and several are suspected to be the underlying cause or to contribute to complications in autoimmune diseases. Mushroom foraging and other outdoor pursuits are recreational. Don't risk your health.

If you are adamantly against wearing clothing that has been chemically treated, it is important to take every precaution to protect yourself. After every hike, always thoroughly check yourself EVERYWHERE! If you can't see a spot, ask a friend to check for you. Yes, even THOSE spots. I hope you have better friends than I.

NOTE: If you have a cat, take the utmost care when using Permethrin. In its liquid state Permethrin can be fatal to felines even in very small amounts. Never treat your clothes indoors. Always apply Permethrin outside in a well-ventilated area, and be sure to let clothes dry completely before wearing them.

Finding Mushrooms as a Beginner

While the prospect may seem daunting, getting started foraging mushrooms is no more difficult than going for a walk with an attentive eye. If you look carefully, you will find mushrooms—not necessarily edible mushrooms, but most certainly a fungus of some sort. Don't let the many thousands of inedible or poisonous "little brown mushrooms" distract you, though: they will only waste your time and yield frustration. Instead, concentrate on the species of mushrooms featured in this book for a better chance of success: your pursuit will be more fruitful and satisfying.

Let your friends know about your new interest. Ask them to inform you of any unusual mushrooms they encounter. I cannot count the number of great mushroom harvests I've had because friends sent a text about some freaky fungus they saw while walking their dog or on their morning run around the lake.

If you're not having any luck on your own, connect with a local mycological club. At least thirty-seven states and three regions have them, as do chapters of the North American Mycological Association and mycology departments in most American universities. These organizations are filled with mycophiles (mushroom lovers) who will gladly offer tutelage and on occasion even company on forays into the field. Just don't expect anyone to give up the location of their patches.

A Word on the Ethics of Foraging

Most mushrooms happened upon in the forest are neither tasty nor likely to be identified by the average person. Collecting a wide variety of unknown fungus is surely going to frustrate you and result in utter failure of your goal of positive identification. When members of the North American Mycoflora Project make scientific collections, we focus on fewer than fifteen species in a day because the great difficulty in determining the specific species can take weeks or even months and may require DNA sequencing to reach a conclusion.

On too many occasions I have found an abandoned pile of wonderfully edible mushrooms that someone picked and presumably decided their identification was too uncertain to risk eating them. While I applaud the choice to err on the side of safety (when in doubt, throw it out), it is disheartening and irritating to find this kind of wanton waste.

Many mushrooms are geotropic, growing to align themselves to keep their gills, pores, or teeth, from which they release their spores, vertical to allow for optimum distribution. Going about the forest toppling every mushroom cap one finds is in no way helpful to the ecosystem.

If you are curious about a mushroom, pick one. ONE. Bring that mushroom home and photograph it from all sides, take a spore print, crack open your field guides, and give it a go. If you find that you just can't make a determination, try posting the photos online in one of many mushroom groups or forums. Facebook has dozens.

The question of ethics in foraging is important for all who harvest from the natural world. Embarking on an activity with the consumption of a resource at its center brings great responsibility. It is easy to become enthralled and absorbed when one finds a good edible to forage, but it is imperative that we all curb our greed in order to protect these resources for future harvests. While it may seem a meaningless practice to leave a good portion of a patch unpicked, the benefits are not confined to that fungal organism. The greater picture of the entire ecosystem of which these fungal fruitbodies are a part is a complex interplay of all the organisms living there. As we come to better understand the role of mycelial connection in the subterranean superhighway, it is clear that ecosystems are far more interactive than we ever imagined. It is our responsibility as stewards to ensure that we are both protecting when we can as well as managing our own impact on the environment as we pursue our activity.

Even though the mushrooms we seek are merely the fruit of the organism and their harvest in no way harms the host, there is evidence that trampling the ground in a patch can result in a thirty- to forty-percent reduction in future fruitings. This detail alone should prompt everyone going out into the wild to tread lightly and practice good stewardship at all times.

The resurgence in popularity of harvesting wild edibles has begun to put a strain on the carrying capacity of natural areas, especially parks and public spaces in and around larger metropolitan sectors. And some people are intent upon making a living from foraging. While I applaud the enterprising spirit, the idea of pitting a natural resource against a profit motive when public land is the source for these products is troubling. Foraged products are not to be sold from public lands. This policy includes charging a fee to guide someone on public lands and harvesting commercial quantities of mushrooms. The more abuse our public lands take, the more likely restrictions or absolute prohibitions on foraging will result. Let's try to not ruin things for each other.

Morels

Yellow Morel (Morchella esculentoides)
and Black Morel (Morchella septentrionalis
or Morchella angusticeps)

Morel mushrooms are probably the most widely harvested of all varieties of wild mushroom species in the United States. The broad distribution of the different species of this genus and the ease of identification contribute to their popularity. In Minnesota, the morel has been granted status as the "official" state mushroom.

Familiarity is evidenced in the many colloquial names given to morels across the country. From sponge mushrooms to molly moochers and merkels or hickory chickens, morels are a choice edible, one of the first to arrive after a long, cold winter. The spring equinox marks the point when winter is done and mushroom season will shortly be at hand. It's my alarm clock, so to speak, reminding me that I must prepare for the arrival of those long-awaited fungal friends. There are boots to dress with waterproofing, knives to sharpen, foraging clothes to treat for ticks, and many other odds and ends to tend to before setting out into the fields and forests.

A scant month later, and black morels will begin reaching up from the depths of the obscured and complex world of the soil. Each sunny day warms the earth a bit more, and the melting snow seeps into the ground, bringing just the right conditions to bear. Avid morel hunters begin really scouting once the nighttime soil temperatures remain above 40 degrees for four days in a row, with a couple days of high temperatures above 70 degrees. Some more aggressive hunters may be out sooner, searching the south-facing slopes where the sun's angle warms the ground more intensely, in hopes of catching some early-season success.

Scouting morel patches in early spring carries an anticipation rivaled by few seasonal events. Step cautiously when checking your patches, as the young mushrooms in their pinning stage can be impossible to see under the leaf litter and other forest debris. Better to return in a few days than risk disturbing the developing fungus.

The morel's honeycomb-pitted cap is a distinct shape and form, and aside from the wrinkled cap species of false morels such as *Verpa bohemica* and *Gyromitra esculenta*, there are no dangerous look-alikes. The false morels are easily distinguished by comparing the ridges and pits of true morels to the wrinkled brain-like appearance of false morels. Regardless of wives' tales, folklore, or cooking tricks, none of the false morels are safely edible.

In Minnesota, we are lucky enough to have two distinctly different morel species to harvest. The early-fruiting black morel, *Morchella septentrionalis*, appears north of the forty-fourth parallel and comes into season three to four weeks ahead of the yellow, or golden morel. More commonly found associated with green ash or among the bigtooth aspen (especially young, dense stands) in the northwestern portion of the state, it is also sparsely distributed as far south as Houston and Winona Counties in the southeast, where it may overlap with *Morchella angusticeps*. This species is virtually indistinguishable from *septentrionalis* aside from being slightly larger, and is widely distributed south of the forty-fifth parallel and east of the Rockies.

The yellow morel, *Morchella esculentoides*, is both larger and likely a more prolific mushroom in Minnesota. Mostly associated with American elms, it can sometimes also be found with green ash and somewhat less often with cottonwood trees in river valleys. Early fruitings of the yellow morel are sometimes gray and were previously considered a different species. DNA analysis, however has laid to rest this myth. I have long theorized, based on observation, that the mycelium produces different-looking fruit bodies throughout the season: gray morels in the early days, yellow morels in the mid-season, and the legendary bigfoot morels in the waning days.

It is not understood why bigfoot morels grow so large, but I have experimented multiple times by leaving a mid-season patch to mature in hopes that it would develop these giants, only to return to find that the mushrooms didn't achieve that hoped-for greatness. As exciting as it is to find the season's first fruiting morels, it can be even more intoxicating to be in the woods when the bigfoots are on. Few harvests can compare to a basket full of bigfoots measuring up to twelve inches, prized for recipes that involve stuffing large caps. Their overdeveloped size doesn't seem to adversely affect their flavor.

Because morels and their host trees have a mycorrhizal relationship (that is, a symbiotic relationship whereby the mushroom mycelium gives nutrients such as minerals and water to the trees in exchange for carbohydrates and sugars created through photosynthesis) and the morels tend to fruit when that host is dead or dying, patches will diminish over time and eventually stop producing altogether. It's good to always be on the lookout for new potential patches to keep your morel harvests strong.

An aside: After many years of finding yellow morels in association with dying elms, I noticed that a particular tree might produce morels for several years and

then suddenly cease as pheasant back mushrooms appeared. I have never found morels around a tree that produced fruitings of pheasant back, leading me to postulate that the mycorrhizal relationship with the morel mycelium has likely reached its conclusion and a saprobic relationship (that is, one where the host organism has died and is being consumed, often for its cellulose) with the pheasant back mycelium ushers in the next phase of decay for the elm trees.

After a spring rain, morels may be coated in sand and all the spore pockets filled with grit. Sometimes a mushroom brush can't clear those crevices, so I usually give my morels a quick rinse and shake under cold water, then lay them on a kitchen towel to dry before cooking or dehydrating.

Recipe: To stuff large morels, trim off the stems and chop them up. Mix some tangy goat cheese with chopped piquanté Peppadew peppers and a generous amount of finely chopped toasted pistachios. Spoon the filling into a plastic or pastry bag so you can pipe it into the mushroom caps. Arrange the stuffed caps in a baking dish, snugging them together. Cover with foil and bake in a 375-degree oven for about 40 minutes, uncovering halfway through. Meanwhile, cook the chopped stems in butter, stirring often until tender, then simmer with some white wine and a splash of heavy cream. Season to taste. Spoon over the tender mushrooms. Garnish with toasted pistachios.

JOURNAL ENTRY

May 21, 2013   Location: REDACTED
Temperature: High 65 degrees—cloudy—.07 precipitation

Traveled south of the Twin Cities metro looking for morels. Temperatures lately have been wildly fluctuating. Only a week ago it was 98 degrees, and we have gotten more than three inches of rain in the past three days. After a couple dozen empty stops, we finally got into a line of elms that were producing nice-sized yellow morels. With hopes lifted and a good start at real numbers filling my baskets, we decided to drive to a spot that tends to hit a bit later in the season, but I was curious if all the rain and the nearly 100-degree day last week would move things along. Sure enough, my hunch paid off, and soon we had filled every basket, bag, and bucket in my truck. With morel season off to a stellar start, we headed home to begin the tedious task of cleaning and cooking or drying our prizes.

Pheasant Backs

Pheasant Back (Cerioporus squamosus)

Sometimes called hawk's wing or dryad's saddle (for their resemblance to a saddle or seat), the pheasant back is an early spring arrival often fruiting alongside morels and in the right habitats can easily be found throughout the mushroom season. The feather-like patterned scales that adorn the top of this fungus appear, as the name suggests, like the back of a hen pheasant. Pheasant back is a bracket or semicircular shelf fungus that can grow to be as large as two feet across. In Minnesota, pheasant backs grow from dying or deceased hardwoods like elm, ash, maple, and box elder trees.

There are no poisonous look-alikes for mature pheasant back specimens, but very young mushrooms may be confusing for the novice. For this reason, I recommend collecting only those that have the distinctive feather patterning on the upper surface and the unmistakable aroma of watermelon rind. Typically, a single cap about the size of your hand is ideal, though larger examples are fine so long as they are tender. Often with this and other polypore, bracket-type mushrooms, on larger specimens the outer edges of the caps are tender and palatable if trimmed away from the tougher inner portions and stems.

Pheasant back is one of the few mushrooms whose flavor profile does not pair particularly well with butter in some preparations. This, coupled with its texture (which may also be reminiscent of a saddle), can make the pheasant back a difficult subject in the kitchen. Sliced very thin, they are a great addition to Asian-style soups, but cut into thin strips, tempura battered, and fried is by far my favorite preparation for this species. While pheasant backs are not considered a top-shelf mushroom among many foragers, they are quite good once one overcomes the expectation that they will taste like other mushrooms. The toughness of some pheasant backs doesn't necessarily come from size but from age. In the early spring, especially in wetter years, when the mushrooms grow very rapidly, even the larger specimens can be soft enough to make a meal. Later in the season, as the spring rains subside, this species will grow more

slowly, and by the time a mushroom reaches larger diameters, it will be older and therefore tougher.

Pheasant back can be dried to grind into powder for use as a dredge, or the dried brackets can be used to make stock. Rehydrating for the fork is not recommended. The farinaceous, or watermelon rind, quality often does not completely cook away, leaving pheasant backs with a flavor some find troublesome in more commonly fungus-friendly cuisines. Still, if in the woods on a beautiful spring day you are skunked by the morel hunt, a large flush of pheasant back can be a very welcome discovery indeed.

Recipe: For a crispy tempura batter, mix ⅔ cup rice or pastry flour, ⅓ cup cornstarch, and 1 teaspoon baking powder in a medium bowl. Whisk in 1 large beaten egg, 1 cup ice-cold water, and a pinch of salt until just blended (some lumps are fine). Dip strips of pheasant back in the batter; deep-fry for about 3 minutes in hot peanut oil. Serve sprinkled with sea salt mixed with matcha green tea powder, tamari, or sweet chili sauce.

JOURNAL ENTRY

May 27, 2011   Location: REDACTED
Temperature: High 64 degrees—cloudy—.22 precipitation

It's been cooler this week. Only in the sixties. Had almost two inches of rain a week ago, and another inch or so over the last few days.

Some days pheasant back is merely a consolation prize for a failed morel hunt, but today the pheasants were beautiful—the perfect size—and everywhere. Unfortunately, I find again that my hunch about morels no longer fruiting on a dead elm after the pheasant back fungus appears to be holding true. One of my early and great morel spots has sprouted a hearty fruiting of pheasants, and not a single tiny morel was to be found. I will check back regularly this season to be sure I haven't just missed the moment.

I'm always intrigued by the interplay between species in nature. The changing of the guard with morels to pheasant back, or the way a certain patch will produce intense flushes of *Russula, Lactarius,* and chanterelles overlapping in timing or sometimes all at once is astonishing.

I am reminded of my buddy Ryan's disdain for pheasants. He told me early in our hunting days that he can't stand the taste of them. I said, "You know, the best thing to do with pheasants is—" at which point he interjected with, "Yeah, leave 'em in the damn woods!"

They're not everyone's cup of tea, but I know folks who collect morels to trade with others for their pheasants. Each to their own, I guess. Now it's time to go deep-fry some tempura-battered pheasants.

Golden Chanterelles

Golden Chanterelle
(Cantharellus cibarius *[complex]*)

Not many experiences can outshine that of coming upon a river of golden caps flowing across the forest floor. The color of egg yolks, the golden chanterelle stands stark against the dull brown of leaf duff. Sometimes when the chanterelle season is strong and the timing is right, you can follow a string of gold for hundreds of yards at a time, picking baskets full of sunshine in a matter of an hour or two.

Chanterelles are one of the most beloved and sought-after mushrooms around the globe. In the Midwest, they occur in association with oak most commonly in the south and with pines in the north. Thanks to the region's broad habitat types, there are likely a half dozen or more species of chanterelle in Minnesota, ranging from the hearty and robust *Cantharellus phasmatis*, a bright yellow–capped, white-stemmed beauty, to the dainty and delicate *Cantharellus cinnabarinus*, a much smaller, brightly colored salmon-pinkish/orange-colored mushroom.

Chanterelles are currently the subject of major taxonomical rearrangement and classification. Taxonomist Anna Gerenday, connected with the nationwide MycoFlora Project, locally supported through the University of Minnesota and the Bell Museum Herbarium, is working to sequence the DNA of a previously undescribed white chanterelle I found in northern Minnesota in mixed hardwoods of birch and bigtooth aspen with scattered oaks. *Cantharellus lateritius*, sometimes called the "smooth chanterelle," is another variety that is likely to be split into multiple taxonomies before all is settled with North American chanterelle species. Similarly, I commonly find in northern areas of Minnesota a chanterelle that may fall under *Cantharellus flavus*. DNA testing will eventually be needed to sort out the details.

The golden chanterelle, with its compelling combination of characteristics, is one of my favorite wild mushrooms to harvest. The rich golden color makes it easily one of the more visually stunning mushrooms, especially once you have collected a basket full of them. Add to the eye-candy aspect the beautiful warm, fruity aroma, and you will find it hard to resist sticking your head in your basket every few seconds to inhale the heady smell of summer. And finally, their habit of growing in great meandering troops makes harvesting a satisfying endeavor.

In the kitchen, the golden chanterelle continues to shine as one of the most delectable edible wild mushrooms. Almost no dish that calls for a mushroom would not be vastly improved by substituting golden chanterelles. Sautéed in butter, salt, and pepper with a splash of white wine and finished with heavy cream, golden chanterelles will make even a common chicken breast a meal fit for royalty.

Chanterelles do have a dangerous look-alike: the jack-o'-lantern (*Omphalotus illudens*), which can be distinguished from chanterelles in several ways. Chanterelles always grow from the ground, have very short, blunted, almost melted-looking gills that fork, and commonly have a sweet, fruity smell reminiscent of apricots. Jack-o'-lanterns always grow in clusters, sometimes dozens from one singular point, and on wood (though they can grow from buried wood or a tree root appearing to grow from the ground) and have distinctly deep, fin- or knifelike gills that do not fork.

Chanterelles will commonly grow in staggering numbers. It's not unusual to pick ten pounds in a short two-hour hunt. Typically, once you find one, you're on the trail of many. Chanterelles can grow in great, winding veins across the forest floor, sometimes breaking for some unknown, unseen underground obstacle, only to pick up again a few yards away. Like the Yellow Brick Road, they meander through the brown leaf duff in a golden thread. Chanterelles are a great choice for introducing children to the wild mushroom hunt as they are so easy to spot and the large numbers make a midsummer hunt very rewarding. Just remember to always inspect each and every one before it goes into the pot so that no mistakes are made in identification.

Recipe: To make a warm salad, toss halved small chanterelles, fresh asparagus spears, and small cubes of butternut squash with olive oil, a sprinkle of sea salt, and some freshly grated nutmeg. Roast at 425 degrees on a parchment-lined baking sheet for 25 minutes or until tender. Arrange over a bed of baby kale, torn dandelion greens, and torn fresh herbs (dill, sage, and/or cilantro). Dress with a drizzle of olive or walnut oil and sherry vinegar.

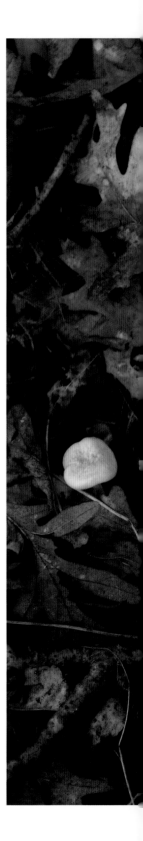

Journal entry

July 27, 2013   Location: REDACTED
Temperature: High 64 degrees—cloudy—.02 precipitation

Much cooler this week than earlier this month, and it made picking so much more comfortable. Not so sweaty and humid. Chanterelles are up in record numbers. I picked seventeen pounds in the open oaks along the bench below the ridge. There were really good flushes of young buttons perfect for sautéing whole. I'll have to pick out a couple handfuls for infusing some vodka for cocktails. Along the bottom on the way back out we came upon a pretty good run of king boletes. Ran out of room in the baskets and backpacks and had to head out early. What a problem to have! Will definitely go back out midweek.

I found an unusual-looking chanterelle which may be a variety or perhaps another species. White fleshed, with a yellow cap surface and a uniformly faintest pale yellowing on the stipe and gills. These mushrooms had a more slender stipe with a slight bulge to the base and were small in comparison to other chanterelles with white flesh that I find.

Chicken of the Woods

Chicken of the Woods
(Laetiporus sulphureus, Laetiporus cincinnatus)

Chicken of the woods, sometimes abbreviated to COW and also commonly known as sulphur shelf, is a widely distributed fungus that separates into two distinct categories in the eastern United States: those growing directly from wood and those appearing to grow from the ground. *Laetiporus sulphureus* and *Laetiporus huroniensis* are the wood growing types, and *Laetiporus cincinnatus* is the species that sprouts from the ground. Once considered a single grouping, *Laetiporus sulphureus* has grown to be a much broader complex of genetically differentiated species: currently six separate species and one varietal type.

One note of caution: avoid any chicken of the woods growing from a conifer. Folklore surrounding this variety suggests it can be a sickener. While mushroom writers do not mention this detail in eastern species, they do note that the eucalyptus-loving COW in the west are to be avoided for this reason. It is probably best to err on the side of caution, but I have personally never run across this *Laetiporus huroniensis* among all the hundreds of pounds of chicken I have harvested over the years.

Chickens can grow in such large clusters and groupings that it's possible to collect more than fifty pounds from one tree in one harvest. As a wood rot fungus, *L. sulphureus* can mostly be found in scars and injuries of oak trees, often high above where a large branch has been broken. *L. sulphureus* is easily distinguished from *L. cincinnatus* by coloration and environment. *L. sulphureus* has a bright orange top with a bright yellow- (sulfur-)colored pore surface below and grows from dead or dying trees, while *L. cinicinnatus* has a more muted salmon-colored top surface and a white pore surface underneath and commonly appears to grow from the ground (in actuality, it is growing from a buried root but sprouts from the earth, which for the beginner can be confusing).

One of the "foolproof four" (see page 14), chickens are easily identifiable with no real look-alikes. The other two similarly colored polypore mushrooms that grow from trees are too woody to be considered edible, do not grow as shelves, and lack the distinctive sulfur-colored pore surface.

In late summer as chicken season begins to kick into high gear, I love the feeling of excitement that is added to my mushroom outings. As chickens can grow in large clusters, the sudden appearance of a bright-orange basketball in the dark forest understory is electrifying. A moderate cluster of chickens is easily spotted at a hundred yards; you'll want to alter your scanning technique when on the stalk. I usually do a side-to-side pan at about six to twenty feet for all those forest floor fungus, and then a long-range pan through the trunks as far as I can see. That bright flash of orange is visible from surprisingly far away, but beware: as the season presses on, the changing fall foliage may begin to trick you with a sprig of sumac or maple leading you on a wild goose chase. But take your time on this fool's errand: perhaps you'll discover some other edible along the way.

Chickens can grow quite high up on their host tree, making their retrieval somewhat challenging, and from below the lighter shade of their bottom sides perfectly camouflages with their sun-dappled under-leaf surroundings. Just remember to keep looking up.

As with their barnyard namesake, young specimens of chicken are the most desirable. These tender morsels (we call them nubbins) can be cooked in a dry pan, adding a touch of oil or butter as they begin to lose their moisture. Chopped coarsely with a splash of white wine and finished with salt, pepper, and fresh chives, the result added to the top of a Caesar salad can scarcely be distinguished from actual chicken. I've even fooled the nieces and nephews with this treatment of chickens. My non-meat-eating friends covet my annual gifts of chickens and rejoice in the years of abundance. Chickens are a wonderful ambassador for wild fungi among the uninitiated and the mushroom phobic.

When harvesting chickens, select the outer portion of each shelf. Taking only these outside bits allows the leftover fungus to drop its spores. I like chicken even when it is a bit older and begins to get woodier; the stringy texture enhances the "chicken-ness" of this fungus. Take care when harvesting chickens: as they become tougher, they can also become more difficult to digest and commonly are full of larvae. Small portions and thorough cooking make for a prudent approach with this polypore, and as with all mushrooms it is wise to test a small bit on your first time eating it.

With their remarkable capacity for holding moisture, chickens are quite weighty and take up a good deal of room in the freezer. These will freeze quite well after being sautéed (see duxelles recipe, page 284).

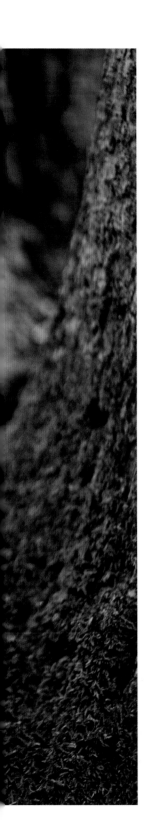

Drying is an acceptable option for long-term storage, but because lengthy rehydration is required to get them back to a palatable texture, this preservation technique should be used only if freezer space isn't available.

Journal entry

May 28, 2013   Location: REDACTED
Temperature: High 70 degrees—raining—.18 precipitation

Overnight temperatures have fallen into the forties and fifties in the past week. The leaves are changing quickly, and chicken of the woods is EVERYWHERE!

The bright orange flush of chickens against the backdrop of fall leaves blanketing the forest floor makes for a spectacular view. We harvested more than sixty-five pounds from six different trees at the "Chicken Farm" (our nickname for the best patch of COW-producing woods I've ever seen). The first two trees we spotted from the truck driving into the property. After collecting those and finding a few more trees with beautiful flushes of fresh, tender chickens, we came upon the mother lode. A large oak trunk about twenty-two inches in diameter broken off at about eight feet high was simply covered in chicken. I think we collected more than twenty pounds from that one tree. Looks like it's going to be a very busy Sunday in the kitchen, but the freezer will be full, and there will be chicken of the woods all winter long.

Oysters

Oyster Mushroom (Pleurotus sp., Pleurotus ostreatus, Pleurotus populinus, Pleurotus pulmonarius)

Oyster mushrooms found in the Midwest are actually a complex of several species: *Pleurotus ostreatus* (the fall or autumn oyster), *Pleurotus populinus* (the aspen oyster—found almost exclusively on quaking aspens but sometimes also on cottonwoods), and *Pleurotus pulmonarius*, a species that is more pale and tends to fruit in the warmer months from spring to summer. One of the most commonly referred-to characteristics of oyster mushrooms is their aroma. Many people describe fresh, wild oysters as having a mild to strong anise (licorice) or sweet almond smell. Of note, cultivated oysters seem to be devoid of this characteristic odor.

Oysters love a wet season. I commonly find *Pleurotus pulmonarius* in huge flushes when we have an unusually wet spring. The pale caps and tendency to fruit gregariously makes *P. pulmonarius* especially easy to spot on overcast or rainy days as they almost glow in the darkened understory, and I often will find a single tree with enough oysters to completely fill my basket and cut short my search with a trek back to the car to stash the bounty. All oysters are favorites of fungus beetles and fungus gnats, which means that early- and late-season specimens, harvested when temperatures are cooler, are more likely spared the ravages of these insects. *P. populinus* can flourish in astounding numbers, covering large sections of standing dead aspens high up on the trunk. I've left many an oyster to the heights and the bugs out of sheer survival instincts. It takes only one or two such attempts to remind oneself that shinnying up a tree with a knife clenched in your teeth in a remote patch of forest with questionable cell service is not a wise endeavor. I like to reassure my wife that I would never be one to attempt such feats of strength.

All three of these species of oysters are equally flavorful and a welcome find on any outing. Oysters' subtle but distinct flavor and robust texture hold up well in soups or sautés, and their ease of cultivation ensures that we can enjoy this

mushroom in a fresh state any time of year. Most local markets carry them in the produce section, and if you're interested in trying your hand at cultivation there are many do-it-yourself kits on the market, several available from online sources, or try Field and Forest Products in Peshtigo, Wisconsin.

Recipe: To make a silky tom kha soup, mix 1 (14-ounce) can unsweetened coconut milk, 2 cups chicken or miso broth, 6 quarter-size slices fresh galangal root or gingerroot, the zest and juice from 1 large lime, and 2 (4-inch) pieces tender lemongrass in a large saucepan. Bring to a boil; reduce the heat and simmer for 10 minutes. Add ½ pound fresh wild oyster mushrooms (torn into bite-size pieces), 1 tablespoon Thai fish sauce, 1 teaspoon sugar, and 1 teaspoon chili-garlic sauce. Simmer for 15 minutes longer; scoop out the galangal or ginger and lemongrass. Serve hot with big handfuls of torn fresh Thai basil and cilantro leaves.

Journal entry

May 25, 2016   Location: REDACTED
Temperature: High 76 degrees—partly cloudy—.33 precipitation

Scouting for morels this morning we ran across a beautiful flush of oyster mushrooms. They were in a strange place as there was very little shade. I was surprised to find them in such an open setting. This is why I always implore my foraging friends to go out often and explore new areas. One never knows what surprise is around the next curve or over the next hill. The coloration of these was somewhat darker, and they were firmer and heartier than I sometimes collect. I typically find this variety of oyster (*Pleurotus populinus*) in the fall more often than the spring, and was delighted to have something to bring home for the kitchen on a day that proved too early for my morel spot. The morels were just too small to harvest. In a week, though, providing they don't get too much rain, they should be ready for the basket. In the meantime, it will be tom kha soup tonight with lots of fresh oyster mushrooms.

Hedgehogs

Hedgehog (Hydnum repandum *and* Hydnum umbilicatum)

The hedgehog mushroom is a delightfully different breed of fungi. These two species of edibles differ from our other cap-type mushrooms (chanterelles, king boletes, and shaggy manes) in a remarkably distinct way. The underside of the cap is completely covered in tiny, tightly packed teeth, or spines. This unusual adaptation for spore dispersal makes the hedgehogs an easy ID even for the novice picker. Sometimes called sweet tooth, hedgehogs have a somewhat milder sweet or fruitlike aroma, much like their cousins the chanterelles.

Hydnum repandum, the larger of the two species, can produce caps the size of your hand, with a thick, dense flesh that makes for an excellent addition to the basket. *Hydnum umbilicatum*, smaller and more fragile, has a darker cap color sometimes appearing a deep, brownish orange. While *H. umbilicatum* is just as tasty as its larger relative, it takes quite a few of them to measure up. In the Midwest, hedgehogs appear in the waning days of chanterelle season, though there is always considerable overlap. The larger species, which prefers oak trees, tends to show itself earlier in mixed hardwoods, with the smaller appearing later and continuing into mid-autumn and more commonly associated with small poplar and various conifer species.

Many guidebooks and cookbooks advise to scrape away the teeth before cooking. This endeavor is completely unnecessary unless you've been sloppy in your harvesting practices and allowed dirt into your basket, in which case it is virtually impossible to evict soil particles from between the hedgehog's teeth. Hedgehogs are more suited to the sauté-and-freeze method of preservation as they do not reconstitute well from drying and lose the fullness of their flavor. However, if you find yourself with an overwhelming bounty of hedgehogs as I have in past years, drying is a fine method if you intend to grind them into mushroom powder.

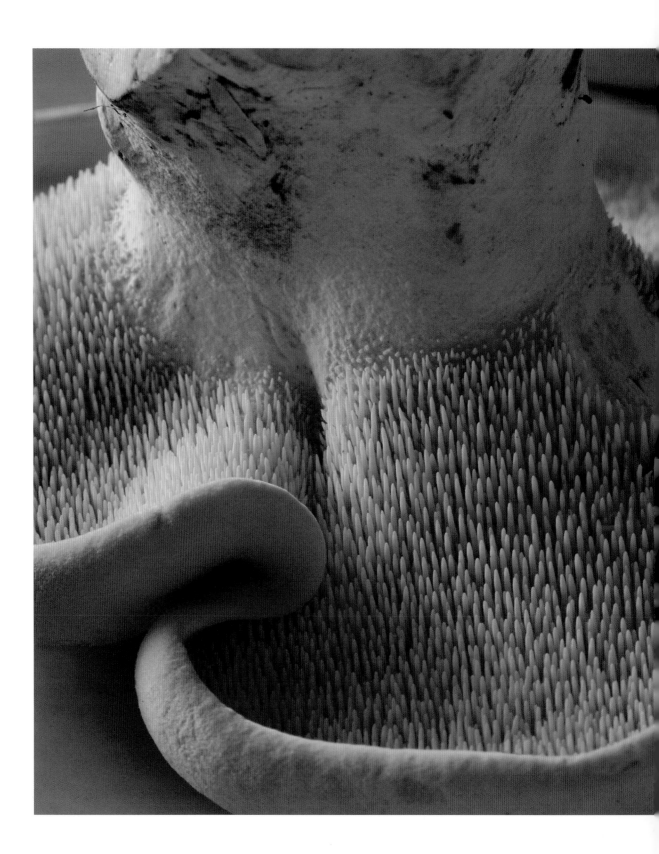

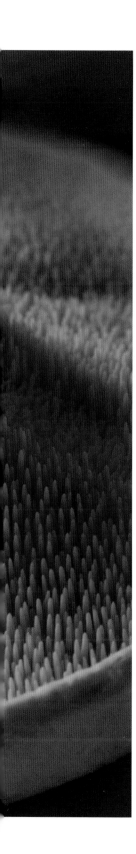

JOURNAL ENTRY
September 1, 2014   Location: REDACTED
Temperature: High 73 degrees—partly cloudy—.05 precipitation

Epic hedgehog hunt today. We picked more than eighteen pounds of hogs. Most were the big, pasty doughboy hogs, and many were wider than a dollar bill. I've had good days picking hogs, but this has been one of the more spectacular in terms of sheer size. All were completely bug free and in beautiful shape. I'll be pickling some of these just for the novelty of having long, toothy spears filling the jars from top to bottom. There were nice quantities of late-season chanterelles, and still quite a few *Boletus pallidus*, along with a few king boletes. And the three five-gallon buckets of black trumpets was a real treat as well. The dehydrators are full, and we sautéed and vacuum-sealed ten pounds of chanterelles. The winter larder is going to be well stocked this year.

Black Trumpets

Black Trumpet (Craterellus cornucopioides,
Craterellus fallax)

Black trumpet, horn of plenty, trumpet of death (as in the French, *trompette de la mort*), and black chanterelles are all names given to this beautiful fungus. I have converted more mycophobes (mushroom haters) with this variety than any other wild mushroom. If I were to pick one species to offer a skeptic, this would be it. It has a lovely, delicate smell reminiscent of the chanterelle's but a bit more floral. If the chicken of the woods is the ambassador of fungi for its texture and acceptable semblance to its namesake, the black trumpet is my pick for flavor. The subtle elements of truffle and earthy sweetness are rich and surprisingly robust for such a delicate mushroom.

David Arora of *Mushrooms Demystified* writes that black trumpets look like black petunias. Aside from their broad variation of shade and tendency toward browns and grays, there is no better description. They look, without a doubt, more floral than fungal. Unlike their flamboyantly colored cousins the chanterelles, black trumpets, with their delicate curving edges and their camouflaging colors, are difficult to spot in the leaf litter beneath the oaks and beech with which they most commonly associate. In the northeastern Laurentian forest of Minnesota, black trumpets are found in association with red oak, though farther north into the boreal forests they are more likely found among the other northern oaks.

Black trumpets grow singly or in troops and at times in vast regiments across the forest floor. With mushrooming friends I have harvested more than thirty-six pounds in one afternoon, a record year for trumpets to be sure, and a sight I have not seen since. We were cleaning and drying trumpets for days. In that patch we usually collect a few pounds several times a year and can almost always count on a meal's worth anytime we venture into those woods between the end of July and November, depending on when the first snow falls. I commonly

find trumpets in the southern region of Minnesota as early as June, but the real bumper crops are in the north.

I pick black trumpets in areas where the mycelium has access to water—not along stream banks or lakeshores, but uphill from a low spot that remains soft and holds water much of the year or along an area that fronts a marshland but has ample mature trees. Trumpets seem to like sphagnum mosses, and some foragers speculate that black trumpets may have a relationship with certain moss species as well. There are many areas in the Midwest where trumpets appear in beautiful carpets of green mosses, which only adds to the enjoyment of finding them and supports this hypothesis. One drawback to my patches in the low areas and those that tend to be mossier is that these areas also host slugs that love to dine on black trumpets as much as I do. They don't eat much, but they do make the cleaning process more tedious, as no one wants to eat a slug.

Black trumpets also rank as one of the top candidates for preserving by drying. A good dehydrator will make quick work of these delicate fungi, and kept in a well-sealed jar they will last for years. Rehydrate according to the instructions for all dehydrated mushrooms (see page 282). Trumpets can be sautéed and frozen, too, but I try to keep my freezer space for those species that don't rehydrate well. Trumpets are a great enhancement to any dish that calls for common button mushrooms. Simply add a portion of trumpets to the recipe—but less than a quarter of the total weight of the button mushrooms, as trumpets can bring an overbearing flavor in larger quantities. They enhance any common dish that calls for mushrooms and really make it shine.

There are no look-alikes to be concerned with, and the related species, which are virtually identical morphologically speaking, are equally as edible. A friend once picked and ate "black trumpets" during morel season, but as it turned out they were devil's urn (*Urnula craterium*). Luckily, it is a harmless species that, while not included in my list of desirables, apparently can be eaten with no ill effects. I'm told, however, that they have a questionable texture. Probably best to avoid.

Recipe: Toss hot cooked rigatoni with a handful of torn black trumpets that have been thoroughly sautéed in extra-virgin olive oil, a handful of chopped garden tomatoes or halved sweet cherry tomatoes, and diced ripe avocado. Season well with sea salt and freshly ground pepper and a shower of shredded fresh basil.

JOURNAL ENTRY
October 19, 2013   Location: REDACTED
Temperature: High 72 degrees—partly cloudy—.0 precipitation

Today started as a virtual bust. A few chanterelles and an occasional hedge-hog opened up the day, and just as we were deciding that the season was all but washed up at our northern location Todd found the mother lode of black trumpets. In five hours four of us picked thirty-six pounds of trumpets. I didn't think this was even possible, and I never imagined that I would see this many black trumpets in one place. All of our dehydrators are full and running. The bulk of the remaining mushrooms will have to be sautéed in batches to be vacuum-sealed and frozen.

[Additional note: Two days later it snowed three inches, ending the mushrooming season for 2013. I've since had many great trumpet harvests, but nothing has compared to the 2013 late-season harvest in northern Minnesota.]

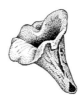

Lobsters

Lobster Mushroom (Hypomyces lactifluorum)

As summer days warm and the heat begins to wear on northern senses, a silent, invisible stalker sets to work. More akin to a mold, this fungus lies in wait for a host to present itself. The lobster mushroom is the standout oddball of fungi discussed in this book. *Hypomyces lactifluorum* is a parasitic fungus that attacks a host mushroom and transforms it into the delicacy that we harvest and enjoy. Along with being a non-mushroom, lobsters also differ from what we typically think of as a mushroom because the parasitized host is completely engulfed in a bright orange (sometimes albino white), dense, thick flesh that utterly obscures the detailed features of the original species to the point that identifying it would likely be impossible without DNA analysis. It is a decidedly odd forest find.

The fungus *Hypomyces lactifluorum* is a cousin of the mold *Hypomyces chrysospermus*, a yellow fungus that attacks bolete species, rendering them grotesque and disgusting. The parasitic fungus that creates the lobster commonly attacks species of *Lactarius* and *Russula* such as *Lactarius piperatus* and *Russula brevipes*, though I have discovered in patches of chanterelles lobsters that I would call unmistakably chanterelle-like, which I find curious. *Lactarius piperatus* is not a common edible as it is quite peppery hot to the tongue, but the transformation performed by this species of *Hypomyces* makes it not only edible but delicious. It is important to note that while it is possible for the *Hypomyces* fungus to parasitize a poisonous host, there have been, to my knowledge, no cases of mushroom poisoning from lobster mushrooms. Perhaps as they completely absorb their host they nullify any toxin, or they are so particular as to parasitize only hosts that are safe for us to consume. Lobsters have been known as an edible for hundreds of years, so in any case something in the process makes them safe to eat.

As a parasite, lobster mushrooms are only as prolific as their hosts, and thankfully here in the Midwest the hosts are quite abundant. When I find patches of *Lactarius piperatus* numbering in the hundreds, I'll think to myself, "Now where is the *Hypomyces*?" One day I happened upon a patch of *L. piperatus* that must have had well over two hundred caps, some nearly as big around as my head, just over the hill from where I picked thirty-eight pounds of lobsters in one afternoon with one of my mushrooming buddies. For whatever reason, this patch had escaped the parasite. There is no rhyme or reason to the fungal world, or at least none that we entirely understand.

Such hefty hauls are not uncommon with lobsters: individual mushrooms may weigh over a pound, and collecting can become more a matter of how much weight you wish to carry rather than how many you can find. Lobsters are not going to be confused with any other mushroom, but new foragers should leave the white specimens in the woods. There is no point in complicating your foraging experience with an unusual example of an edible. I have only one patch that regularly produces ghost lobsters, as we call them, and only a few per year, so you're not going to be missing out on a haul by leaving these anomalies behind.

The lobster mushrooms' commonly associated hosts appear to be mycorrhizal partners with oak trees; consequently, your search for this species should be focused in this forest type. I find that the lobsters in my most prolific patches tend to like a less heavy leaf duff and often fruit from clumps of sphagnum moss under open oak-canopied forests along the sides of steep ravines where the soil holds moisture or where the hilltop just begins to slope toward the valley.

In the kitchen, lobsters are a delight: sturdy and easy to clean. I just put them in a colander, take them to the backyard, spray them with the garden hose to knock off the determined bits of forest debris, and then take a vegetable brush to them in the sink. They hold up well to a good scrubbing, and they don't readily absorb water, making for a quick prep.

They can be dried in quarter-inch slices, preferably in a dehydrator. They are slow to dry, and the remarkably fishy aroma they produce will attract a cloud of flies. Never dehydrate mushrooms indoors. As with other mushrooms, drying will intensify the lobsters' flavor, and I prefer this method of preserving lobsters for this very reason. I enjoy a whole braised lobster when fresh, but rehydrated and added to soups and sauces or dried and ground to a powder for dredging is how most of my lobsters are used.

Journal entry

August 28, 2014   Location: REDACTED
Temperature: High 72 degrees—partly cloudy—.02 precipitation

Had a great day in the woods with lobsters, hens, chicken, chestnut, and *Boletus pallidus*, and a monster haul of black trumpets. Final weight in trumpets was nearly the same as the weight of our lobster collection of twenty-six pounds! The lobsters popped up in our most prolific king bolete patch. It's early for kings, but I like to visit my patches at other times to see what's happening there, and today that practice really paid off. Acres of lobsters, prime for the picking. I'll be really interested to see what the king bolete harvest is like this year. [See journal entry for king boletes (page 93) for more on the 2014 harvest.]

King Boletes

King Bolete (Boletus edulis *[complex]*)

The king bolete: there simply isn't a better name for this mushroom. *King* pretty much sums it up, though it goes by many other monikers around the world: penny bun in Britain, porcini in Italy, cèpe in France, and Steinpilz in Germany. King boletes are known and coveted the world over because they are so tasty. Were they more easily identified by the casual picker, they might even be prized beyond beloved morels.

I have two reliable patches for kings, one in Minnesota's southeastern region and one in its northeastern region. Even so, the total harvest in a given year is quite variable. My northern patch, by far the more prolific of the two, has been known to produce close to a hundred pounds in just a few days of picking, with flushes in the fall around the middle of September.

The *Boletus edulis* complex is currently in so much flux that any in-depth discussion of taxonomy is pointless. All the same, it is vitally important to take great caution when learning new varieties of mushrooms. Let me again stress that failure to be certain of a mushroom's edibility can destroy your life if not end it.

Now that I've put the fear of organ failure and mortuaries prominently in your mind, let's talk about the rules of edible boletes for the novice forager. The first thing to know when delving into the kingdom of the king bolete is to NEVER eat a blue- or greenish-staining bolete. (There are wonderfully delicious exceptions to this rule, but NOT for the novice picker.) "Blue staining" means that when you cut into or break the flesh of the cap or stem, the flesh color changes to a blue or bluish hue. The change can be very subtle, as in *Boletus pallidus*, which can be fickle in its shift to blue and sometimes doesn't shift at all or only changes in a slightly brownish way. Or it can be extraordinary, as in *Gyroporus cyanescens*, commonly known as the "blue-staining bolete," which shifts from a crisp white to a brilliant cobalt or indigo blue in a few seconds, one of the most dynamic oxidizing displays in the mushroom world. It is important to observe even the slightest change in color when determining a mushroom's edibility.

Second, avoid all of the *Leccinum* species. These mushrooms have what appear to be tiny singed or burnt hairs along their stem. (While there are some delightful edible *Leccinum*, they are, again, not for the novice picker.)

Finally, never eat a bolete with a pore surface that is any shade of red to orange or bright yellow. The most dangerously poisonous boletes, such as *Rubroboletus satanas*, fall into this category and are to be avoided most diligently.

Now, what to look for when picking king boletes. I usually describe them as resembling hamburger buns, or maybe slider buns. A king bolete typically will have a somewhat bulbous base, especially when young. It will have a white underside pore surface that becomes pale yellow to olive colored with age. The flesh of the stem as well as the cap is white and will not stain, or change color, when cut or bruised. The stem will have a netlike or weblike pattern called reticulation around it, sometimes more pronounced at the top nearest the cap. The surface of the stem will be white or occasionally brownish. Finally, the cap flesh will taste mild and not unpleasant, with no bitterness. To test, pinch off a small piece of the cap about the size of a raisin and pop it in your mouth, chew it in the front of your mouth, and then spit it out. If it's bitter, leave it be; if it's not, and all the other characteristics are present, put it in your basket and look for its friends.

I start to check my southern patch in early July. This patch sometimes produces five to fifteen pounds of mushrooms in the middle of the month. An early-fruiting patch for kings is quite a treat, but I tend to compete with the fungus gnats and other critters here more than in my northern, later-flushing patch. In either location, an intervening rain can completely ruin a harvest if the bolete mold, *Hypomyces chrysospermus*, strikes. This parasitic mold appears like a white dust or powder and eventually envelopes the entire mushroom, turning yellow and then brown as the whole mess decays. Sometimes the spread of *Hypomyces* can be so rapid that mushrooms left one afternoon, rained upon overnight, and checked the very next day will have already fallen prey to the mold. The eternal risky proposition: whether to leave mushrooms in the woods to grow a bit more. Fungus-loving insects, parasitic molds, hungry animals, and of course other foragers are all part of the ecosystem, which is why it pays to have a number of patches to pick.

King boletes are hearty, rich, earthy, and meaty mushrooms that can act as a stand-in for meat or as a flavor enhancer alongside it in a lasagna.

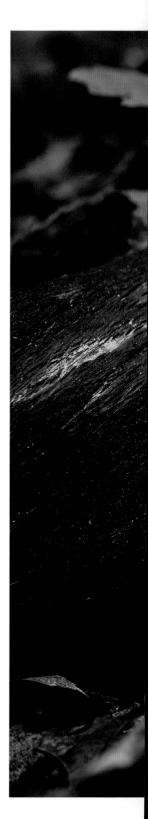

They make the ultimate ravioli stuffing with your favorite cheese and a bit of shallot. The king bolete offers robust flavor, especially when dried, that can be overpowering if not used sparingly, but there is no dish that calls for mushrooms that won't be vastly improved by adding the king of boletes.

JOURNAL ENTRY
August 29, 2014   Location: REDACTED
Temperature: High 73 degrees—partly cloudy—.75 precipitation

Light rain, on and off all day. Mushrooms have been everywhere. The last few days of hunting Todd and I have picked over fifty pounds of chicken of the woods, nearly twenty pounds of hen of the woods, five pounds of lobsters, two pounds of chanterelles, one pound of chestnut boletes, three pounds of *Boletus pallidus*, and a few kings.

Today . . . one hundred pounds of king boletes. I'm exhausted, sore, and absolutely giddy! I have to buy a second dehydrator.

Shaggy Manes

Shaggy Mane (Coprinus comatus)

Sometimes referred to as lawyer's wig in Canada, shaggy mane is one of the only edible mushrooms that is "self-digesting." As a self-deliquescent fungus (meaning they turn themselves to liquid), shaggy manes are quite delicate. They begin self-digesting from the bottom of their bullet-shaped caps and rapidly deteriorate upward. One must move quickly to prepare this fresh mushroom, as harvesting only seems to hurry along the process of self-destruction. To preserve, it is best to cook and freeze this species. Drying by dehydrator is an option, but this mushroom will only melt into black, inky liquid if left to dry on open-air screens.

Shaggy manes are often found in organically rich soil and commonly appear gregariously in large groups in wood chips, lawns, and grassy or open areas. Although they may arrive in summer, I find that shaggies tend to really come up with the fall rains. Once the dense soil has gained some moisture, shaggy manes can push their way through some remarkably difficult ground—even the asphalt of a park path or driveway, a surprising achievement for such a delicate, soft mushroom that melts away. With miles of mycelium in a single cubic inch of soil, the fungus can exert enormous turgor pressure, especially considering the vast reach of mycelial bodies. Some estimates suggest that a growing fungal body can produce pressures upward of one to two hundred pounds per square inch. That's a lot of muscle.

Shaggy manes can be used to make a natural ink. Simply place several shaggy caps in a glass bowl and cover loosely. Set in a garage or exterior building, as the deliquescing mushrooms will begin to smell. When the caps have dissolved into liquid, strain through a fine mesh. Add one teaspoon whole cloves to every cup of liquid, and then boil to reduce it to the desired ink consistency. Cool the ink, strain out the cloves, and store in an airtight, dark bottle for up to twelve months. Extend the shelf life of this ink by adding ethyl alcohol to achieve a ten percent by volume measure (in other words, if you have made five ounces of ink, add a half ounce of alcohol).

Shaggy mane is undergoing some taxonomical restructuring. The genus *Coprinus* suggests that shaggy mane contains coprine, a chemical used in making Antabuse, a drug prescribed to treat severe alcoholism. Antabuse blocks enzymes involved in metabolizing alcohol, creating very unpleasant effects including severe vomiting, vertigo, shortness of breath, and a pounding, rapid heart rate. Thanks to this lexicographical link, many assume that shaggies should be avoided if one consumes alcohol. I'm here to dispel this myth—even though doing so may increase the chances of my patches being picked.

Some people may have had an adverse experience with this mushroom unrelated to alcohol and rested the blame on the easiest target. These inky mushrooms do not react with alcohol. Still, it is important to note some other auto-deliquescing fungus do contain coprine, so it is wise to avoid alcohol even days before or after consuming them, as the sensitivity can persist for some time.

As one of the "foolproof four" (see page 14), shaggy mane is relatively easy to identify. However, I like to point out to new foragers that *Chlorophyllum molybdites*, "the green puker," has several characteristics in common with shaggy mane. The puker also loves open grass such as lawns, and it has a scaly cap surface as well. Because of this cursory likeness, novices should pick shaggies only from a grouping where at least some mushrooms are showing signs of self-digestion.

Shaggy mane has a less robust flavor profile than some other wild mushrooms, pairing nicely with milder foods like eggs. A favorite preparation is to carefully stuff the manes' bullet-shaped caps with a fine grated cheese, wrap with bacon, and broil them in the oven. Alternatively, brush the stuffed caps with egg wash, roll in panko, and fry them in a skillet. Shaggies, which sometimes taste mildly of asparagus, also make a fantastic cream of mushroom soup, highlighting that grassy flavor coupled with a wonderfully earthy savor (see page 237).

JOURNAL ENTRY

October 8, 2013   Location: REDACTED
Temperature: High 68 degrees—partly cloudy—.00 precipitation

Honey mushrooms are up everywhere. I picked some smaller caps for pickling and found a large patch of aborted *entolomas* that were perfect and dry. After collecting a couple nice hens, on my way out I happened upon a beautiful patch of shaggy mane and collected enough for a hearty batch of cream of mushroom soup. With all the fall leaves on the ground around this flush of shaggies, I don't think I've ever seen a more photogenic group. What a treat: I so often find these growing in good numbers in places that aren't wise to collect from.

Lion's Manes

Lion's Mane (Hericium americanum,
Hericium coralloides, Hericium erinaceus)

As the first hints of autumn begin to appear, we see the last straggling chanterelles. Where before they stood in large troops laced through the trees in rivers of gold, now there are only singles and the odd couple left like refugees. Along with the increasing rains come the first toothed mushrooms: lion's mane, also sometimes called monkey head, bear's head, or waterfall mushrooms. I begin checking a decaying old log, the harbinger of *Hericium* season. Once I see this spot produce, I know to go and check my others. If you are lucky enough to find a patch (in this case, a tree), it can be counted on to produce with some consistency for years to come.

A collection of fungus fall within the genus *Hericium*. The three species found in the Midwest are all edible and, in fact, considered choice. Two are quite similar in appearance: *H. americanum* and *H. coralloides* are branching in their growth, sometimes vastly so. I once encountered growths of *H. coralloides* in Arkansas that had tunneled through a fallen log so completely that my pickings from that singular tree resulted in a bounty of more than twenty-five pounds. The third is different in general shape: *H. erinaceus* fruits singularly, in a concentrated, unbranched body with much longer teeth. I have rarely found this species much larger than a softball, though there are records of them growing larger than a football. Commonly found on beech, oak, and maple, *H. erinaceus* feeds on dying heartwood and fruits through some fracture in the host such as a broken limb, a split in the trunk due to wind stress, or an old knothole. Thus the mycelium reaches the outer surface of the tree to sprout its mushroom and spread its spores.

All three species of *Hericium* are equally prized. *H. erinaceus* can be a bit chewier than the other two, but thinner slices and longer cooking will usually coax out its tender tastiness. The two branching varieties are of equal flavor and texture, but I find *H. coralloides* far more frequently than *H. americanum*.

This group of fungus is one of the more richly flavored. Little more than attentive cooking and salt and pepper are needed to produce a fine treat. Many report that these toothed mushrooms have a texture and flavor reminiscent of lobster or crab, though I feel they are only subtly similar.

JOURNAL ENTRY

September 5, 2016   Location: REDACTED
Temperature: High 65 degrees—sunny—.00 precipitation

Went to check the bolete patch and came up empty. Still seeing lots of *Amanita muscaria* around, so the kings should be popping any day now. On the way out I stopped in to check the dead maple by the cemetery and, sure enough, the *Hericium coralloides* was prime and perfect. I couldn't have hit it on a better day. Six pounds from three nice clusters. Since these were out I decided to check our other spots, and they were producing as well. Another eight pounds from two other trees for a total of fourteen pounds for the day. I'll be making lion's mane fried rice and cooking the rest for freezing. It's going to be another busy night in the kitchen.

Giant Puffballs

Giant Puffball (Calvatia gigantea)

Commonly known as the giant puffball, *Calvatia gigantea* is the largest but only one of several species of edible puffballs. Puffballs belong to the Gastero-mycetes class of fungi, which develop their spores internally, hence the prefix *gastero*, as in "stomach." As the mushroom grows, the internally held spores mature and eventually the outer sclera, or skin, becomes brittle and begins to slough away, leaving the trillions of spores to be dispersed by the elements and whatever passersby, animal or human, come in contact with the fruit body.

One spot I regularly find puffballs is a grassy slope with a bit of exposed earth here and there. Viewed from a distance when the puffballs are fruiting, the hillside sometimes looks like it's scattered with skulls, conjuring the gravedigger scene from *Hamlet*: white orbs cast about like bleached skulls eroded from the hillside by the ages.

The giant puffball is quite unusual in shape compared to what we normally think of as "mushrooms": it ranges in size from golf ball small to larger than a basketball, is sometimes lobed or splitting, and swells into large, amorphous lumps of nearly unrecognizable marshmallow-hued fungus. One spring while out photographing warblers at a local bird sanctuary, I spied what I thought to be an old, broken Styrofoam cooler in the bushes. I pushed into the ground cover to retrieve the "trash," only to discover it was an overgrown giant puffball. While the average giant puffball is grapefruit- to soccer ball–sized, there are records of five-foot and fifty-pound examples. My cooler-sized puffball measured only a diminutive twenty-two inches. I find the most desirable size for the kitch-en is that of a softball up to a soccer ball. Only collect specimens that are firm and pure white inside.

Giant puffballs are often the first wild mushroom that new foragers are willing to try due to ease of identification and lack of dangerous look-alikes. Unfortunately, puffballs are not the most convincing ambassadors of the wild mushroom's culinary value. Though not robust or deeply complex as the king

bolete, the simple puffball has much going for it. Like tofu, the puffball takes on the flavors it is combined with, and its soft, tender, but not slimy texture is one that even the most vehement mushroom haters find approachable. Sliced as "steaks," dipped in egg and panko, then fried crisp, giant puffball perfectly replaces eggplant in a baked Parmesan.

As a child I gathered these odd orbs with my siblings, sometimes finding a flush of ten to fifteen mushrooms in grassy fields or on the edges of the forest near our home. Back then we simply sliced the puffballs, fried them in butter until golden brown, and usually ate them as fast as they came out of the pan.

As with most mushrooms, giant puffballs can be dehydrated and ground to a powder, but this species doesn't perform well rehydrated or frozen. (Parmesan steaks would likely be just fine if cooked to crisp before freezing.) The dried powder makes a great dredge for breading fried chicken or for adding depth to soups and stock.

One important safety note: early—or egg-stage—*Amanitas* can sometimes look like young puffballs. Any small puffball harvested from the ground that shows discoloration or a shaped pattern in the flesh when sliced should be discarded. Many *Amanita* species can be dangerous, and one or two can prove deadly. Additionally, while many species of puffballs are edible, the focus here is on *Calvatia gigantea*, the giant puffball. Its large size at maturity is easily identified with no fear of confusing it with the *Amanitas*. If you're interested in exploring other puffballs, be sure to reference your identification resources and forage ahead. Some say that the species *Calvatia cyathiformis* is the stand-out flavor champion of all the puffballs.

Journal entry

September 29, 2008   Location: REDACTED
Temperature: High 60 degrees—partly cloudy—.09 precipitation

Out birding today and found three nice giant puffballs. The largest was just smaller than a volleyball, and the other two were grapefruit-sized. Just the size I like them. These will make a perfect baked Parmesan, and I will have leftovers for drying into dredging powder. I have to remember to check back in this spot. I don't often hunt mushrooms in these woods, so when puffball season rolls around again I can hopefully score more.

Hen of the Woods

Hen of the Woods (Grifola frondosa)

Also known as maitake in Japan and ram's head or sheep's head in North America, hen of the woods is very different from the common "cap"-type mushrooms. Widely distributed throughout the eastern United States, in Minnesota hens are most commonly found in close association with oak trees. In mid-August I begin keeping my mushroom eyes peeled for the first signs of hens. They usually begin fruiting with the red oaks earlier in the season and follow with the white and bur oak fruitings later. It is not uncommon to find several large florets within yards of one another, at times even associated with the same tree. Any area known to produce hen of the woods could easily fruit multiple times in a season.

Hens can grow quite large, and their labyrinthine layers and folds can hold any number of species of insects, spiders, rodents, or even small snakes and lizards. I once shook a rather startled field mouse from imagined safety among the fronds of the *frondosa*, depositing the stunned critter onto the forest floor with a plop and a shower of roly polies. None the worse for wear, he scurried away, and I made off with my spoils.

Hen of the woods is an unambitious parasite that causes a white butt rot in the trees with which it is associated. Though the fungus is evidently a saprobe—meaning it derives its nutrition from decaying organisms, the host tree in this case—the work is quite clearly a long-term effort. I know of people who have been collecting hens from the same tree for more than two decades, illustrating the wisdom of knowing your patches and checking them regularly within the season. Many hens will fruit at the base of the same tree, if not in the exact same spot, for many years, sometimes skipping a year or two, only to fruit again when the mushroom gods decide.

Hen of the woods are remarkably diverse in their colorations as well as shape and size. I have picked specimens from the same woods on the same day with hues ranging from golden browns to grays to almost bleached white, all of them fresh and relative in size and age—which, again, shows that color is never a good identifier in mushrooms. While they reportedly can grow to as large as a hundred pounds in Japan, I have personally never witnessed a hen weighing in at more than twenty-nine pounds. While I would not disbelieve the claims of forty-plus-pounds from examples collected here in the Midwest, the average fresh specimen is likely to weigh somewhere closer to fifteen pounds.

Hens often grow around and encapsulate anything in their surroundings: leaves, branches, bark, and so on. This, coupled with their tendency to collect critters and debris, makes them a bit of a chore to clean at times. I try to assess the quality of my finds before picking and usually leave the crustier examples in the woods to do their fungal duties or just trim the nice, tender fronds I want for the kitchen rather than collecting the whole mushroom. Much of the center stalk of hen of the woods will be fairly tough and not worthy of the fork. On the other hand, it does make for a rather good mushroom stock if you're that industrious. I have sometimes saved all the stalks from a season, freezing them until there's enough to make it worth the effort to boil for stock. Harvesting these large frilly fruitings can be a bit cumbersome; to collect them whole, use a long fillet knife to reach underneath and cut at the base instead of tearing it away from the mycelium.

As with all polypores, it is imperative to be cautious when eating a new species. Remember to try only a small amount, one or two bites, the first time you consume any new mushroom. While hens are very common and widely cultivated (usually marketed as maitake) throughout the United States, this species is known to create gastrointestinal irritation in some people. While not dangerous, such an outcome is, nonetheless, unpleasant.

Hen of the woods is generally one of the most approachable of Minnesota's wild mushrooms. It has a very rich, earthy, and woodsy flavor, but it also carries a strong nutty character that elevates this mushroom from its earthly origins and makes it suitable for many dishes that require a solid flavor base. From jerky to risotto, hen of the woods is a cornerstone of the kitchen-friendly mushrooms. For a real treat, try our recipe for tikka masala (page 212) using hens as a replacement for the chicken of the woods.

JOURNAL ENTRY

August 29, 2013   Location: REDACTED

Temperature: High 95 degrees—partly cloudy—.33 precipitation

Six days in a row of 90-degree weather. I've been in heaven, though all my mushrooming friends are complaining about the heat. Honestly, I would have been as well except unbelievably I found three huge hen of the woods today. Side by side, they are beautiful. One is nearly white, one is gray, and one quite brown. I would never have expected to find them in this hot, dry weather. We haven't had rain to speak of since the 1.3 inches on the sixth of this month. These were the bonus to the monumental haul of thirty-eight pounds of lobsters earlier today. Foraging is fantastic.

· · · · ·

These thirteen species of edible mushrooms are by no means the only delicious options available to the dedicated forager. If you've caught the bug, as I'm sure many of you will, take your time and use the guidelines for gathering data and mushrooms (pages 19–39) and you will be well on your way to expanding your repertoire of fine fungal fare.

A Coming of (Mushroom) Age

I grew up, as Michael describes, an American who loved her tuna noodle casserole (I'm from the West Coast, so nary a hot dish at my house). Don't get me wrong: my mother was an adventurous and skilled cook for her time. But she was a product of a good farm cook and the 1950s convenience food era—and cream of mushroom soup was the "it girl" of easy sauces. I'm also part of the waning years of corporate test kitchens, setting forth with my newly minted diploma and degree in "consumer service in food" to encourage legions of cooks to find new ways with packaged foods. A bowl of cream of mushroom soup, made with reconstituted nonfat dry milk, of course, shared with my dad for Saturday lunch was delicious; a steaming dish of that tuna noodle casserole the ultimate in cozy comfort.

But beyond canned soup, mushrooms at my house were a special treat. Nothing more than a box of store-bought buttons, these cultured white mushrooms (forget baby portobellos or even a stray shiitake) were always served sautéed in most likely modern margarine, to eat with a grilled steak, also a treat. And they were expensive, so our family of five shared a meager bowl like it was meaty gold, one small spoonful per plate. They did play a role in my aunt Janet's beef stroganoff stew (my uncle Charlie was a butcher), but just a bit part as compared to the hearty chunks of beef (see page 259 for her recipe). This was a company dish, so again, something to look forward to.

As time passed, my acquaintances with edible fungi became much broader and sophisticated. Time spent working in San Francisco expanded my palate to all sorts of Asian oddities, including a world of dried and fresh mushrooms I'd never before set eyes upon. I studied classical French cooking in Paris, worshipping the elusive truffle but deeply appreciating Escoffier's love of *cèpes* and *girolles*. (Escoffier worked on a theory of identifying a fifth taste he called "deliciousness," what we now know are the glutamates in foods like mushrooms that impart a salty-meatiness to a dish.) I gained a German father-in-law who foraged for morels in the Midwest and Rocky Mountains. I traveled in Italy at the peak of porcini season, when farmers parked their trucks alongside country roads, truck beds groaning with mountains of fresh king boletes. And as the New American Cuisine took off, I ate plate upon plate of warm wild mushroom salads—a mixed bag of whatever a forager sold to the chef, sautéed and tossed with tangles of bitter greens and from-the-skillet vinaigrettes, a mingling of mushroom juices, tangy vinegars, and brilliant oils.

Working on this book, guided by a master at finding these amazing fruits of the forest and fields, is just one more step in my love affair with mushrooms. I now consider myself a card-carrying mycophile. And one important thing that Michael and I are in total agreement on is that the French are right: the very best way with an untamed mushroom is a hot skillet with some good butter and an attentive cook.

A Cook's Advice

I'm not fussy about things like using salted versus unsalted butter or measuring every little ingredient perfectly. But I am particular about quality ingredients—from where and from how far away they've traveled to my kitchen. I do believe in ingredients that originate close to home, but having grown up in the desert Southwest I couldn't do without avocados or citrus on my table, even though they don't grow anywhere close to where I currently reside. The spices I'm obsessed with travel many more miles than I ever will, but they have permanent residence in my favorite seasoning drawer. Welcome to my eclectic home kitchen, where I'm less about following recipe rules and more of a technique gal—paying closer attention to what food looks like as it cooks, how it smells, and finally how it tastes. In the daily grind of getting meals on the table, it's relaxing to settle into the rhythm of chopping, stirring, even washing a pan or two.

For our purposes here, paying special attention to your hard-gained wild harvest, I've played with flavors, listened to local stories, and distilled as much as I could into the mushrooms. If a skillet of sliced golden chanterelles or hedge-hogs are crisping up around the edges in a bubbling pool of butter, if they smell so good it's hard to get them to a plate without snitching one, and if once you've sprinkled them with a couple of pinches of good salt and a hefty grind of black pepper they taste wonderful, what's to argue about?

I fight my tightly controlled culinary training, forcing myself to loosen up—settling into more organic ways, taking more cues from the wild ingredients. I've let them tame me rather than the other way around. I encourage you to use your hands more, tearing up mushrooms and fresh herbs, using fewer gadgets, trusting your senses and kitchen intuition. And as all recipes are just guidelines, you should let loose and make each one your own. My favorite collections are filled with my own penciled notes of how I tweaked recipes to my own taste or tailored them to what I had on hand that particular day.

I rarely offer amounts for salt and pepper, trusting that you'll season and taste your food along the way. I do admit to being a bit of a geek about both salt and pepper, always grinding whole peppercorns or rocky sea salt. I confess to hoarding an embarrassingly large collection of smoked, garlic-infused, and spiced salt and pepper blends. But my daily mainstays are a coarse sparkling kosher salt and robust black Tellicherry peppercorns in a favorite copper grinder. And I cook almost exclusively with a good extra-virgin olive oil (spend a few more bucks for one with character—it's worth it) or creamery butter from dairies not far from my neighborhood. I use an eclectic collection of skillets, from restaurant-style stainless steel and nonstick to cast iron, but all are at least twelve inches in diameter so there's plenty of room to let mushrooms brown rather than steam. I heat pans well before adding oil or butter, and I like to lightly toast seasonings—even salt and freshly ground pepper if it makes sense to do so—for a few seconds before adding food.

The best kitchen practices with wild mushrooms are pretty simple: cook them until they are very tender and browned and even a bit crisped around the edges. Undercooked mushrooms may cause digestive upset for some and in my opinion just don't taste as good as they can. Many of the species featured here have a high water content, so allow them to release their juices, then slowly become golden: that caramelization is the key to developing the best flavor. Others, like chicken of the woods or lobsters, are denser and can be treated more like meat—grilling slices, stir-frying chunks, baking them in casseroles. And wild mushrooms are generally nutrient dense. Though levels vary from species to species, they have a high protein content, offer significant amounts of B vitamins, can be a source of vitamin D if they're exposed to sunlight, and provide an assortment of beneficial minerals.

This collection of recipes is inspired by where we live—and where we're walking in the woods, going to farmers' markets, or shopping at local co-op groceries—and what we do in our leisure time as it relates to good eating. We are not full-fledged (or particularly informed) foragers for other edibles: we're just passionate about mushrooms. I've taken my kitchen cues from my team and let the mushrooms lead me to easy ways to savor what we find. We know what we experience, but we also know that no matter where you call home you will find many of the same foods, and with a little bit of the knowledge we're sharing, hopefully you'll happen upon your own trove of these intriguing fungi.

A Note About Substitutions

Please know that many varieties of interesting mushrooms are now cultivated and available alongside locally foraged mushrooms throughout the warmth of late spring and into the chilly air of autumn. Feel free to experiment and swap in what you can get your hands on if your own mushroom stalking turns up a bust (or, in Michael's parlance, you get skunked). I've purchased beautiful fresh oyster mushrooms in my favorite Asian markets and found gorgeous bunches of hen of the woods flown in from the West Coast, and there's never a shortage of shiitakes. As you cook beyond *Agaricus bisporus* (those now ubiquitous cultivated white and brown button mushrooms), you'll begin to discern differences in flavor and how a specific variety melds with other ingredients in a recipe. Take your cooking on a freestyle spin whenever you can. The loveliest aspect of cooking with mushrooms is they can deservedly star in a dish or be the subtle undertone to a recipe, bringing that much-extolled infusion of what the Japanese call *umami*, a savory, irresistible deliciousness.

We'll expand on the best kitchen practices for handling each mushroom species as we meander our way through the coming seasons of hunting, cooking, and of course sitting down to enjoy the pleasurable work of bringing wild mushrooms to your table.

Basic Kitchen Wisdom FAQs

Trimming? As Michael underscores, paying close attention to how you harvest any mushroom will make your kitchen prep easier and faster. Leave the forest floor behind rather than carry it into your kitchen sink. Trim stems and stubbornly embedded dirt, along with any bug trails. If there's any sign of mold on a mushroom, best to discard it whole as the mold could permeate the entire mushroom.

To wash or not? A good, efficient rinse is fine; just don't soak them. I concur with Michael that species like lobsters need an aggressive spray of water and a good vegetable brush to clean out dirty crevices, while chanterelles or boletes may need only a quick run under the faucet. Morels need to be swished around a bit in a bowl of water or you may end up sandblasting your teeth during what otherwise would be a lovely meal.

Driving bugs away? Untamed mushrooms live in the wild, along with lots of other creatures. But most of those tiny invaders you may not see at first really dislike the cold. Once you arrive home, place your haul, loosely covered with a lightly dampened paper towel, in large covered containers. Chill for a few hours, and you'll be surprised by the appearance of tiny bugs or slugs clinging to the toweling at the top of the containers. Lift them out and quietly dispatch.

Stash for how long? Mushrooms are highly perishable, so it's best to be ready to process them (dehydrate, cook and freeze, or transform into a wonderful meal) as soon as you arrive home. But you can buy some time with proper short-term storage. The same large containers you might use to drive away critters lurking within a cache of mushrooms work well for temporary chilled storage. Line the containers with paper towels, arrange the mushrooms carefully in layers separated with more toweling, and be careful not to overload so nothing gets crushed. Top with a layer of lightly dampened towels and tightly cover for up to a few days. Denser mushrooms like lobsters and chicken or hen of the woods will store a bit longer, while shaggy manes need to be attended to immediately.

Best cooking techniques? All wild mushrooms should be cooked until they are very tender. King boletes are sometimes very thinly sliced, dressed with a vinaigrette, and served raw, but that's a rare exception as far as I'm concerned. Quickly searing or dry sautéing before adding oil, butter, wine, or cream can intensify the unique flavor of some species, while others benefit from a flavorful fat to enhance their native taste. Many wild mushroom experts believe in the "less is more" rule, allowing each mushroom's unique flavor to shine. And I'm on board with that to a point, but I also believe that mushrooms can be that addictive savory "it" factor that takes other foods to another level—combinations that are a high-flying sum of the individual parts.

Morels, with their crenellated surface, are a sanctuary for gritty dirt. Gently swish them in a couple changes of ice water (don't soak them) until the water is clear. Very cold water will keep them firm. Michael takes the time to check them, one by one, for bugs that may be hiding in the hollow stipe—going so far as to use a cotton swab to clear out the very tiniest morels. Dry them on paper toweling, trim the end of the stems, then slice them up or cook them whole.

Pheasant backs can get quite large. If they're small, just trim the stems and slice them; earlier in the spring they tend to be more tender no matter the size. Large caps can become the first grilled "veggie" burgers of the season. If it's late spring and they've grown quite large (plate size or bigger), trim the outer, more tender edge of the caps to sauté and turn into duxelles (see page 284) or pickle them.

Golden chanterelles can harbor dirt in their gills, especially if picked after a summer rain: a soft vegetable brush and a quick rinse (they have a high moisture content already, so avoid too much water) is usually enough to clean them up. Chanterelles fairly glow in the woods, and their flavor does the same in just about any way you cook them. Trim the stems (save the trimmings for mushroom stock) and slice or halve them to sauté in a large, hot skillet in good butter. Bugs can work their way up the stems and are easily discovered by halving the mushrooms lengthwise. A few bug trails are fine, but if they are too extensive, discard the mushroom. You can decide how discriminating you want to be.

Chicken of the woods are best cleaned by wiping carefully with a damp cloth rather than giving them a swim, as they will absorb water easily. Young COW is very tender and breaks easily into chunks, or you can slice each scalloped layer where it connects to the main core. Trim off any woody edges (nearer the core) or sections that have softened or look deteriorated. Then slice the pieces into strips, chop them into chunks, or break larger pieces into cutlets (about the size of a small hand) that can be grilled or breaded like a chicken breast.

Oysters are mildly flavored, tailor-made for sautéing, stir-frying, or deep-frying in tempura batter as they easily adopt enhancing seasonings. Their chewier texture complements crisper or more creamy partners in recipes. They are best preserved as a duxelles as they lose their personality when dried.

Hedgehogs, with their toothy undercarriage, need a little care when harvesting since dirt can be caught up in the textured surface. A soft brush is the best way to loosen any soil that's splashed up during a summer shower or from ordinary forest traffic. Slowly sautéed until very tender, they're subtly delicious and meaty. Like oysters, they offer an inviting palette for a wide range of seasonings while contributing their own flavor-rounding essence.

Black trumpets are woodsy and sweet. They do appear delicate and should be inspected for bugs and handled gently. They can withstand a light shower of water to remove dust and grit; drain them well on a clean kitchen towel. They have a stunning appearance and very rich flavor, making them an excellent choice as an accent mushroom. Trumpets meld well with other, milder species. I find their richness satisfying in small amounts.

Lobsters have a very firm white interior flesh and are more resistant to bugs. Trim away brown spots or parts of their cap that are heavily embedded with dirt as you harvest them (though some of that might be removed with a good brushing in the kitchen). Rinse them well. Their mild flavor is really enhanced by sautéing, frying, or grilling—or braised with boldly flavored ingredients. Their brilliant orange exterior will dye foods or tint poaching water a purplish-orange, which can be used for dying wool or handmade paper a faint flamingo pink to a deeper red. I'm fascinated by the seashell-like appearance a lobster lobe can have—an ironic nod to the lobster's faint hint of shellfish taste.

King boletes are quite impressive in the woods, living up to their name in both appearance and flavor. If you harvested them carefully, cutting their fat stems close to the ground and brushing away loose dirt in the field, you won't need to do much once you arrive home. The caps will get slimy if you rinse them too thoroughly, so a soft brush is best. Check them for bug infestation by looking under the cap and slicing them in half—and don't cry if you need to cut away a few nibbled-upon parts. Quickly sautéed, king boletes offer a meaty texture and deep, earthy flavor that tastes like autumn to me.

Shaggy mane need to be handled carefully and quickly. Because they begin to deteriorate almost immediately after picking, gently brush off any dirt rather than rinsing, and cook them up. They're best in simple recipes like omelets, creamy soups, or pastas. If you've gathered more than you can eat at once, go ahead and make a batch of duxelles for the freezer.

Lion's mane, with their furry appearance, are truly surprising. Sometimes described as flavor-soaking sponges, they don't dry well but are quite good sliced and quickly sautéed in butter until very crisp and browned. I note a slight bitterness in them, but that disappears once they're golden and balanced with a little vinegar or stirred into creamy scrambled eggs.

Giant puffballs are a fun but sometimes startling discovery. Once you've cut through their taproot and carried them home, brush them with a soft cloth or rinse under running water. Be sure the inside flesh is marshmallow-white and firm; if they have turned greenish-yellow and spongy, they're too old to eat. Slice off the root end and inspect for any bug damage. If puffballs are larger than six inches across, they tend to have a leathery outer skin that's easily peeled once you slice them. Very mildly flavored, puffballs are the ultimate canvas for bold seasonings, crumb coatings, or just a good stir-fry in hot butter. I've cut them into french-fry sticks, dipped them in beaten egg and then bread crumbs spiked with lobster mushroom powder, and deep-fried them until very crisp. No ketch-up needed.

Hen of the woods has lots of nature-made places for small bugs or slugs to hide. Once you've carted a good-sized hen back to the kitchen, carefully break off petals (or leaves or fronds) and trim away the softer core (the part that was attached to the tree). Be watchful for anything that moves, rinsing with a steady stream of water and then draining the hen well on a kitchen towel. I like to tear hens into chunks rather than chop them with a knife. For a little drama, try grilling or roasting large clusters until tender and crispy, then serve drizzled with a seasonal herb pesto.

spring equinox

butter-braised spring asparagus & morels

serves 4

1 pound fresh asparagus spears

8 tablespoons butter, divided

½ pound fresh morel mushrooms, halved if large

½ small red onion, cut into thin slivers

coarse salt and freshly ground pepper to taste

½ teaspoon grated lemon zest

2 tablespoons fresh lemon juice

¼ cup torn or roughly chopped fresh dill, tarragon, lovage, or chervil, plus some whole leaves

Snap off the tough bottoms of the asparagus spears. If using large, thick asparagus peel the lower ends with a vegetable peeler. Set aside.

Melt 2 tablespoons butter in a wide skillet over medium-high heat. Add the mushrooms and red onion; season with salt and pepper. Sauté about 6 minutes or until just tender. Scrape into a bowl.

Melt remaining 6 tablespoons butter in skillet; add asparagus in a single layer and season with salt and pepper. Add ½ cup water, cover, and bring to a simmer. Cook about 3 minutes or until the asparagus is firm-tender and still bright green. Remove asparagus from pan and arrange on a serving platter.

Increase heat to high; simmer pan juices briskly about 1 minute or until reduced. Stir in lemon zest and juice. Turn off heat; stir in torn herbs. Spoon morels and red onion over the asparagus, along with the pan juices. Scatter a few fresh herb leaves on top.

kitchen notes

Save the tough ends of the asparagus if you're inclined toward chilled spring soups. Simmer them in a good chicken or mushroom broth with some garlic chives or watercress and some chopped new potatoes. Purée the soup, add a splash of cream and some chopped herbs, salt, and pepper, and chill. Serve in small cups with a spoonful of sautéed morels and toasted croutons. This recipe is a good one for playing with fresh herbs: I always like tarragon in the spring, and dill is an easy partner. But if you've got a spray of lovage, with its celery-like taste, in your garden or delicate chervil, toss them in.

rye berry risotto with tender peas & mushrooms

serves 6

5 tablespoons butter, divided

½ pound fresh morel mushrooms, rinsed well and sliced

coarse salt and freshly ground pepper to taste

6 cups low-sodium chicken broth

1 medium onion, finely chopped

2 cloves garlic, crushed in a garlic press

1 cup uncooked rye berries

1½ cups shelled fresh English peas

2–3 tablespoons chopped or torn fresh mint

fresh pea shoots, if you'd like

Melt 1 tablespoon butter in a large heavy skillet over medium-high heat. Add the mushrooms; season with salt and pepper. Sauté about 6 minutes or until mushrooms start to brown around the edges. Scrape into a bowl.

Meanwhile, pour broth into a medium saucepan; bring to a simmer. Melt 2 tablespoons butter in skillet over medium-high heat. Add onion and garlic; season with salt and pepper. Cook, stirring often, for 6 to 8 minutes or until very tender. Scrape into the bowl with the mushrooms.

Melt remaining 2 tablespoons butter in skillet over medium heat. Add rye berries; stir to coat. Cook and stir for about 3 minutes or until rye is lightly toasted. Add broth by the cupful, stirring occasionally, allowing the rye to absorb broth before adding more. Continue until all the broth is used and the rye is tender, which should take about 45 minutes. Stir in peas during the last 5 minutes of cooking.

Stir morel-onion mixture into risotto. Cook a few minutes longer, until heated through. Serve in shallow bowls, scattered with mint and some pea shoots.

kitchen notes

Rye berries, ground into flour, are the go-to grain for sturdy Finnish breads. But whole rye makes a toothsome risotto that's high in fiber and lots of minerals. Its unique flavor pairs well with spring peas and rich morels. Boost its earthiness with mushroom stock, if you've got some on hand, and swirl a spoonful of tangy crème fraîche into each serving.

spring turkey piccata with morels

serves 4

olive oil

½ pound fresh morel mushrooms, rinsed well and halved or sliced if large

coarse salt and freshly ground pepper to taste

¼ cup all-purpose flour

1¼ pounds turkey or chicken cutlets

½ cup chicken stock

3 tablespoons butter

1 tablespoon fresh lemon juice

1 tablespoon chopped fresh flat-leaf parsley, lemon thyme, or basil

1 tablespoon small capers

fresh lemon wedges

Heat 1 tablespoon oil in a large heavy skillet over medium-high heat. Add the mushrooms; season with salt and pepper. Sauté about 6 minutes or until tender.

Meanwhile, mix flour, salt, and pepper in a shallow dish. Dredge turkey cutlets until well coated.

Remove mushrooms from skillet to a bowl. Add 2 tablespoons oil to pan; cook turkey in batches for 2 to 3 minutes per side or until no longer pink in center. Remove to a serving platter and keep warm.

Add stock to pan, stirring to loosen up the browned bits. Bring to a boil; cook until reduced by half. Stir in the butter, lemon juice, parsley, and capers. Spoon mushrooms and sauce over the turkey and serve with lemon wedges.

kitchen notes

If you've got a bird hunter in the house, you may have truly wild spring turkey in your fridge. If you do, slice a boned breast into ¼- to ⅓-inch-thick slices to dredge in the seasoned flour.

grilled lake trout with a mess of morels

serves 4

3 cloves unpeeled garlic

1½ teaspoons cumin seed

½ cup packed fresh parsley sprigs

⅓ cup packed fresh cilantro sprigs

½ cup extra-virgin olive oil, divided

1 large lemon, zested and juiced

1½ teaspoons smoked paprika

1 teaspoon ground *ras el hanout*

coarse salt and ground cayenne to taste

1¼ pounds fresh lake trout fillets with skin, cut into 4 pieces

4 ounces fresh morel mushrooms, sliced

spicy microgreens (turnip, broccoli, kohlrabi, kale, purslane, and/or amaranth)

fresh lemon wedges

Heat grill to medium-high heat.

Toast the garlic cloves in a dry medium skillet over medium heat for 6 to 8 minutes or until the skins blacken. Let cool for a few minutes, then squeeze roasted garlic out of their skins. Meanwhile, toast the cumin seed for a few minutes, just until fragrant.

Place the garlic, cumin seed, parsley, cilantro, and ⅓ cup oil in a small food processor fitted with the chopping blade. Pulse several times until ingredients begin to blend. Add the lemon zest, lemon juice, paprika, and *ras el hanout*. Process until the sauce is well blended. Season with salt and cayenne. Set aside.

Lightly brush the fish with some of the remaining oil; season with salt and cayenne. Place on the grill; cook about 10 minutes, turning once, or until no longer translucent in the center.

While the fish is cooking, heat the last of the oil in the skillet over medium-high heat. Add the morels; season with salt and cayenne. Cook, stirring frequently, for about 5 minutes or until tender.

Serve the grilled fish with the morels, sprinkled with some microgreens, with small spoonfuls of the sauce and lemon wedges.

kitchen notes

This herbal, slightly smoky sauce is a variation of *chermoula*, a lively condiment from North Africa. Look for *ras el hanout* where specialty dry spice blends are sold; it's a heady mixture of warm spices like cardamom, clove, cinnamon, nutmeg, and coriander. The combination will vary from place to place, sometimes including hot chiles, dried rosebud, fennel seed, fenugreek, or grains of paradise (see page 287). I really like the slightly exotic, sweetish edge it adds to a fresh green herb purée—and it's luscious with simply grilled fish, especially nice with the richness of the morels. Stash away leftovers in a jar in the fridge for up to two weeks.

maple-roasted beets & greens with morels

serves 4

1 pound baby red beets with tops

1 pound baby golden beets with tops

1 bunch (6 ounces) baby white turnips with tops

¼ cup real maple syrup or honey

¼ cup olive oil

2 tablespoons white balsamic or apple cider vinegar

3 cloves garlic, finely chopped

coarse salt and freshly ground pepper to taste

4 ounces fresh morel mushrooms, rinsed well and halved if large

Heat oven to 425 degrees. Trim the small tender greens from the beets and turnips; place in a bowl of cool water. Scrub the beets to remove any dirt (no need to peel), then halve them. Arrange in a large roasting pan with the turnips.

Mix maple syrup, oil, vinegar, and garlic; evenly pour over vegetables and toss gently to coat. Season with salt and pepper. Place in oven; roast for 20 minutes.

Carefully stir mushrooms into vegetables; continue roasting for another 20 minutes or until the vegetables are fully tender. Drain the reserved greens and toss with warm vegetables and pan juices.

kitchen notes

Small bunches of newly pulled beets and baby white turnips, complete with their topknots of curly-edged greens, are a treat in the spring and early summer. A combination of golden and deep crimson beets, a handful of turnips, and spring morels are not only visually beautiful but their mixed earthiness is balanced with a light sweet-tart glaze of maple syrup and vinegar. Give the harder root vegetables a head start in the oven, then toss in the mushrooms about halfway through the roasting time. Add a spoonful of crumbly, tangy blue cheese to each serving for a rich edge.

mushroom, fava & forest ramp succotash

serves 3

1 pound fresh fava pods

5 slices thick-sliced applewood-smoked bacon, cut crosswise into ¼-inch pieces

1½ cups chopped or torn small fresh pheasant back mushrooms

4–6 ramps, including the green tops, cut into 1-inch pieces

freshly ground pepper to taste

chopped fresh parsley

hot pepper sauce, if you'd like

Pop open the fava pods and remove the beans. Blanch beans in boiling salted water, then squeeze each bean so the waxy skin bursts open and the lime green interior bean slips out. Gather them in a small bowl.

Cook the bacon in a large heavy skillet over medium-high heat until crisp. Remove from pan, leaving the fat behind. Add the mushrooms and ramps to the skillet. Sauté for 5 minutes or until tender. Add the fava beans to the pan and cook a few minutes longer. Sprinkle generously with pepper, parsley, and bacon pieces; serve with a good shake of hot pepper sauce.

kitchen notes

Fresh fava beans take a little fussing, but they're worth it. They have an affinity for other spring ingredients like pheasant backs and pungent ramps (wild leeks), the colors and flavors melding beautifully. I'm lucky to get ramps from friends or local foragers, who often find them when searching for morels. But you can sub in leeks (use one large) or green onions if need be. This dish obviously isn't a traditional succotash with corn and lima beans, but you could toss in some fresh sweet corn later in the summer and play with other kinds of mushrooms or beans. My favorite way to eat this is straight out of the pan, spooned over a thick slice of toasted and buttered country-style rye bread, topped with a soft-cooked egg and a good sprinkle of flaky sea salt.

orange-glazed morels & leafy radishes

serves 4

2 pounds fresh radishes with green tops

¾ pound fresh morel mushrooms, rinsed and drained well

3 tablespoons butter, divided

coarse salt and freshly ground pepper to taste

1 tablespoon olive oil

3 large shallots, thinly sliced

½ cup freshly squeezed orange juice

fresh oregano leaves to taste

Trim the greens from the radishes, leaving a little stem on each one. Tear up or chop the greens; set aside. Cut radishes in half or quarters depending on their size. Halve or slice the mushrooms.

Melt 1 tablespoon butter in a large heavy skillet over medium-high heat. Add the radish greens; season with salt and pepper. Sauté about 2 minutes or until wilted; remove to a small bowl.

Melt remaining butter in skillet and add oil. Add the radishes, mushrooms, and shallots. Sauté about 6 minutes or until radishes and mushrooms begin to brown. Pour in orange juice; bring to a boil and cook about 2 minutes or until radishes are just tender. Stir in the radish greens and oregano; season with salt and pepper. Serve warm.

kitchen notes

Radishes are what I think of as an instant gratification garden crop. They're happily among the first vegetables to be planted and harvested—and are fantastically sweet, spicy, and crunchy all at once. I love the variety you can find at spring farmers' markets, where they can appear in a rainbow of colors. But don't relegate them to just the salad bowl; the roots, along with their peppery green tops, are tamed a bit when quickly sautéed with forest morels. But if morels elude you, swap in some chopped pheasant backs. Either way, this partnership of flavors works well with grilled steak.

tangle of spring greens with warm morels & lentils

serves 4

for the vinaigrette

⅓ cup extra-virgin olive oil

1 tablespoon chopped fresh chives

1 tablespoon Dijon mustard

1 medium lemon, zested and juiced

coarse salt and freshly ground pepper to taste

for the salad

1 cup uncooked French lentils (Le Puy or small green lentils)

2 tablespoons olive oil

½ cup sliced small garlic scapes or 3–4 cloves garlic, finely chopped

½ pound (4 cups) fresh morel mushrooms, rinsed well and halved

coarse salt and freshly ground pepper to taste

6 cups mixed baby greens and watercress

1½ cups fresh sugar snap peas, some sliced and some left whole

¾ cup sliced fresh radishes

⅓ cup torn fresh tarragon leaves

garlic chive blossoms, if you have them

Whisk vinaigrette ingredients together until thick.

To cook the lentils, place them in a medium saucepan with 2½ cups water. Bring to a boil; reduce heat and cook for about 25 minutes or until tender. Drain well; toss with a couple spoonfuls of vinaigrette.

Meanwhile, heat 2 tablespoons oil in a large skillet over medium-high heat. Sauté the garlic scapes and mushrooms for 8 minutes or until tender. Season with salt and pepper.

Toss the greens with the peas and radishes. Arrange on 4 plates. Spoon lentils and mushroom mixture on top. Drizzle with the remaining vinaigrette and sprinkle with the tarragon and chive blossoms.

kitchen notes

Salad greens switch-ups celebrate whatever limey-green spring ingredients you find while out on the hunt for morels. The sugar snap peas can be left raw or you can toss them in with the mushrooms and garlic scapes, but keeping them crisp with the other greens in contrast to the tenderness of the lentils and mushrooms is nice.

This salad is a good template for playing with fledgling garden herbs: toss in a handful of whatever herbs with the other leafy greens. If you include herbal bursts of flavor in the heart of the salad you can keep the dressing really simple: a few good shakes of red wine vinegar and your best olive oil is all you need.

sautéed fiddleheads & morels with wild greens

serves 4

½ pound tender dandelion leaves, torn

¼ cup torn fresh tarragon leaves

1 large handful wild garlic mustard greens, if you stumble upon any in the field

6 ounces freshly picked fiddlehead ferns, trimmed

2 tablespoons olive oil

2 large cloves garlic, very thinly sliced

½ pound fresh morel mushrooms, rinsed well and halved or sliced if large

coarse salt and freshly ground pepper to taste

3 tablespoons sherry or red wine vinegar

Place dandelion greens, tarragon, and mustard greens in a large, shallow serving bowl.

Rinse the fiddleheads in a couple changes of water; place in a steamer basket and steam for 8 minutes.

Meanwhile, heat oil in a large skillet over medium-high heat. Add the garlic and mushrooms; season with salt and pepper. Sauté for about 5 minutes, then toss in the steamed fiddleheads. Cook and stir for another 4 minutes or until mushrooms and fiddleheads are tender. Stir in vinegar; bring to a boil.

Remove skillet from heat; spoon mushroom mixture and pan juices over greens. Gently toss salad and serve warm.

kitchen notes

Remove the papery sheath-like bits from the young ferns and precook them by steaming just until crisp-tender. They have a grassy flavor with a mild nuttiness and a texture that's reminiscent of asparagus. Dennis picks these in a shady part of his backyard, where they come up year after year. I generally find dandelion greens into the summer at my local co-op, but springtime is prime for gathering them in your yard if you don't spray your lawn. Same goes for garlic mustard greens, with their broad, heart-shaped leaves; most people regard these as pesky weeds. Pick small, tender leaves in the coolness of spring; soak them in cool water to perk them up if they wilt a little before getting to the kitchen. The roots of the mustard greens are faintly spicy like horseradish.

Make a few cups of crunchy croutons by tossing rough chunks of grainy bread in a large skillet with garlic oil and flaky sea salt. Serve alongside the salads.

fishing opener walleye with spring mushrooms

serves 4

1 cup unbleached all-purpose flour, seasoned with salt and freshly ground pepper or a dash of cayenne

2 large eggs, lightly beaten

1 cup plain dried bread crumbs or panko bread crumbs

1 cup cornflake crumbs

1 teaspoon garlic salt

4 (5-ounce) fresh walleye fillets

¼ cup olive oil

½ pound fresh morels, sliced, or 1½ cups coarsely chopped small fresh pheasant back mushrooms

coarse salt and freshly ground pepper to taste

fresh lemon wedges

Tarragon Tartar Sauce (at right), if you'd like

Place seasoned flour in a shallow dish. Place beaten eggs in a second dish. Mix the bread crumbs, cornflake crumbs, and garlic salt in a third dish.

Dredge fish in flour, shaking off any excess. Dredge in egg, then coat with the coarser crumb mixture. Lay fillets on a rimmed baking sheet (you can do this ahead of time; just keep the fish chilled).

Heat oil in a large heavy skillet over medium-high heat. Add fish to hot oil, working in batches if needed. Cook about 8 minutes, turning them once, until golden brown and crisp. Place fish on a serving plate; cover with foil.

Add mushrooms to skillet; cook and stir for about 8 minutes or until mushrooms are tender and start to brown. Season with salt and pepper. Serve fish topped with mushrooms, with lemon wedges and tartar sauce.

Tarragon Tartar Sauce: Mix 1 cup good-quality mayonnaise, ¼ cup sweet pickle relish, 2 tablespoons finely chopped shallot, 2 tablespoons small well-drained capers, 2 tablespoons Dijon mustard, 2 tablespoons chopped fresh tarragon, 1 tablespoon finely chopped fresh parsley, and a squeeze of lemon juice. If you have time, cover and refrigerate for a few hours to allow flavors to blend.

kitchen notes

This adaption echoes lots of home-brewed versions of shore lunch. Passionate anglers who head for the lakes in the spring have strong opinions on the best way to cook up their catches. My husband keeps things pretty simple; I can't help myself, adding a few herbs and a dash of garlic—so this is a hybrid of my family's way around a frypan. I'm highlighting walleye fillets—the holy grail for many fisherman—but depending on the water, midwestern fisherfolk will haul in northern pike, large and smallmouth bass, lake trout, and lots of panfish like crappies, perch, and sunfish. Spooning sautéed spring morels or pheasant backs over the crispy fish fillets is a bonus, especially with a spoonful of a creamy tarragon-infused tartar sauce.

On another day, bake the coated fish fillets drizzled with oil in a 425-degree oven for about 15 minutes or until no longer translucent in center. Serve on crusty rolls with the tartar sauce for a lakeside lunch on the dock.

faux chicken salad with herbal aioli

serves 6

for the salad

½ pound fresh pheasant back mushrooms (or chicken of the woods, later in the summer), trimmed and broken into large chunks

1 cup chopped celery

½ cup chopped cashews

3 green onions, chopped

for the aioli

¾ cup homemade or jarred mayonnaise

1 tablespoon Dijon mustard

¼ cup chopped fresh tarragon, dill, chives, or chervil

1½ teaspoons grated lemon zest

1 tablespoon fresh lemon juice

2 cloves garlic, finely chopped

coarse salt and freshly ground pepper to taste

for serving

toasted grainy bread

watercress or baby greens, avocado, tomatoes, melon

Place mushroom chunks in a large steamer basket; set inside a Dutch oven with 1 inch of water over high heat. Cover and steam for about 5 minutes or until very tender. Cool; chop and place in a medium bowl.

Add the celery, nuts, and onions to mushrooms. Whisk together the aioli ingredients and stir into the mushroom mixture until everything is well coated.

Sandwich the salad between slices of toasted bread, topped with watercress, or spoon onto baby greens with sliced avocado and ripe summer tomatoes or melon.

kitchen notes

A real chicken salad is a warm-weather staple, for portable picnic sandwiches, stuffed into juicy heirloom tomatoes, or tossed with whatever lettuces are ready to be picked. Using meaty pheasant backs (or chicken of the woods) as a salad base works really well. But you could also cube a giant puffball mushroom or some lobsters, brown them in a skillet, then stir them up with the herbal mayonnaise to fill soft hoagie rolls or a crusty baguette, topped with some pickled carrot, thinly sliced cucumber, or red onion—a faux lobster roll or Vietnamese *bánh mì*.

summer solstice

bacon-wrapped mushroom & vegetable skewers with dill
serves 8 to 10

½ cup olive oil

¼ cup chopped fresh dill

1 clove garlic, finely chopped

freshly ground lemon pepper
to taste

½ pound fresh oyster,
hedgehog, and/or medium-size
king bolete mushrooms (later in
the season)

3 medium dill pickles, cut
into 1-inch chunks

16 cherry tomatoes (red and
yellow)

20 strips (1 pound) thinly sliced
bacon, cut in half crosswise

fresh lemon wedges

Heat grill to medium. Mix oil, dill, garlic, and ground pepper together in a small bowl. Tear oyster mushrooms into 2-inch pieces. Leave other mushrooms whole unless their caps are larger than 1½ inches across, then cut them in half.

Wrap each piece of mushroom and pickle and the tomatoes with a half slice of bacon. Thread 3 to 4 pieces onto bamboo skewers. Brush with the flavored oil.

Grill the skewers, turning a few times, for about 10 minutes or until the bacon is crisp and the vegetables are tender. Serve with fresh lemon.

kitchen notes
Pheasant backs would be a great sub in this recipe; wrap nice chunks from the tender edges of the caps in the bacon and pop them on the grill.

golden panfish with mushroom-caper butter

serves 4

⅓ cup olive oil, divided, plus more as needed

½ pound fresh chanterelle, hedgehog, or king bolete mushrooms, sliced

coarse salt and freshly ground pepper to taste

4 (1-pound) whole dressed panfish (crappie, sunfish, perch, or bluegills or small ocean fish like dorade)

unbleached all-purpose flour

⅓ cup butter

1½ cups flat-leaf parsley leaves

¼ cup small capers

1–2 tablespoons malt vinegar

Heat 1 tablespoon oil in a large cast-iron or heavy nonstick skillet over medium-high heat. Add the mushrooms; season with salt and pepper. Sauté for about 8 minutes or until tender and browned around the edges. Remove to a plate.

Dry the fish well and lightly dust with flour. Sprinkle inside and out with salt and pepper.

Heat the skillet over high heat. Add the rest of the oil and allow it to heat up. Carefully add the fish, in batches, to the pan. Cook for 8 to 10 minutes, turning once, until cooked through and skin is crisp. Remove to dinner plates and keep warm.

Wipe out the pan with a paper towel. Add the butter and melt it over medium-high heat. Add the parsley leaves; cook for a minute or two or until crispy. Remove with a slotted spoon to drain on paper towels.

Pour the butter into a dish, let cool briefly, and stir in the capers and malt vinegar. Serve the fish with the mushrooms and with the butter-caper sauce spooned over each serving. Sprinkle with the crisp parsley.

kitchen notes
If you're an angler, you already know the basics of getting a fish ready for the pan: cleaning, removing the gills, and scaling. But if you're more familiar with cooking skinless fish fillets, ask your fishmonger (or your fisher person) to dress the fish for you. Not everyone is a fan of crispy fish skin, but pan-frying in a screamingly hot skillet is an easy way to achieve it, while cooking the fish on the bone ensures that the meat stays moist and super flavorful. Eat the skin if you like, or peel it back and lift the meat off the bones (have a bowl on the table for scraps). Sautéed mushrooms are a natural late-summer partner with panfish. I like their meaty texture contrasted with the tender fish.

dockside crawfish & lobster mushroom boil

serves 8

¼ cup pickling spices

3 tablespoons crab boil seasoning

½ cup fine sea salt

2½ pounds small red and Yukon gold potatoes

4–5 ears sweet corn, husked and chopped into 2-inch pieces

1 pound fresh lobster mushrooms, thickly sliced

8 pounds live crayfish, thoroughly rinsed (discard any that aren't moving)

chopped fresh tarragon and parsley

lots of fresh lemon wedges, melted butter, and hot pepper sauce or Papa's Cocktail Sauce (at right)

Fill a large (12- to 16-quart) pot with 2 gallons water; bring to a boil. Add the spices, crab boil, and salt. Reduce heat to medium-low and simmer for 10 minutes.

Add the potatoes; cover and simmer for 10 minutes. Add the corn and mushrooms; cover and simmer for another 10 minutes. Lift vegetables out with a large slotted spoon to a large bowl.

Add the crayfish to the pot; cover and cook about 3 minutes. Turn off heat and let the pan sit, covered, for 10 minutes. Drain pot. Pour the crayfish out on a butcher paper–lined table; spoon the vegetables out alongside. Sprinkle with chopped herbs, and set out large bowls of lemon wedges and melted butter and bottles of hot sauce or dishes of cocktail sauce.

To eat, twist the tail from the head of the crayfish, sucking meat from the head if you'd like. Otherwise, peel back some of the shell from the tail, then pinch near the end to release the meat from the shell. Dip into butter or cocktail sauce.

Papa's Cocktail Sauce: Mix 2 cups ketchup, ½ cup prepared horseradish (grated, not creamy), freshly squeezed lemon juice, and Tabasco hot sauce to taste in a medium bowl.

kitchen notes

Crawfish, crayfish, crawdads, mudbugs . . . I know them as sneaky buggers who like to nip at live fish hanging in a basket from our dock. But every summer I have the fleeting thought of actually dipping minnow baskets into the lake to intentionally trap enough for a messy supper lakeside—a midwestern nod to a Swedish summer solstice picnic tradition.

Sub in chanterelles if you haven't gathered any lobsters. Including mushrooms in a crawfish boil isn't unusual, but wild ones really hold their own dunked into a bowl of melted butter. "Papa" is my dad, who taught my boys how to make his cocktail sauce for Dungeness crab. The making of the sauce has been a tradition since the kids were old enough to pay attention. It's pretty basic but terrific with boiled shrimp, crab, and crayfish. I'm actually sharing just an outline for Papa's incendiary version; it's all about adding and mixing till it tastes right to you.

farmland mushroom-filled pork burgers

serves 6

1 pound fresh oyster, hedgehog, or giant puffball mushrooms, trimmed and chopped

⅓ cup finely chopped red onion

olive oil

freshly ground pepper to taste

1¼ pounds ground pork

½ cup finely chopped fresh herb mix of flat-leaf parsley, sage, and rosemary

1 teaspoon king bolete (porcini) powder (see page 282)

2 teaspoons Worcestershire sauce

1 egg, lightly beaten

coarse salt to taste

toasted brioche rolls

spicy mayonnaise, caramelized onions, and heirloom tomatoes, if you'd like

Heat oven to 425 degrees. Line a rimmed baking sheet with parchment. Spread out mushrooms on baking sheet; sprinkle with onion and drizzle with 2 tablespoons oil. Season with ground pepper. Roast for 15 to 20 minutes or until tender.

Place mushroom-onion mixture in a food processor fit with the metal blade. Process until very fine. Cool.

Mix the pork, mushroom mixture, herbs, mushroom powder, Worcestershire, egg, and salt and pepper until blended, but don't overwork it. Using damp hands, form the mixture into 6 patties (they will be soft); place on a baking sheet. Chill for an hour to firm up the patties.

Broil the burgers for 8 to 10 minutes, turning once. Or bake at 425 degrees for about 10 minutes, then finish them in a hot skillet with a splash of oil or on the grill to get a golden-brown crust. Serve sandwiched on toasted brioche rolls with some spicy mayonnaise, caramelized onions, and thickly sliced heirloom tomatoes.

kitchen notes

Mixing roasted mushrooms into ground meat for better burgers has been a big deal on college campuses, where dining halls and students are embracing initiatives to lighten up menus while still getting a fill of their favorites. The mushroom-meat combo is super moist and flavorful—and a terrific way to use mushroom scraps, stems, etc. If you have some Freezer Wild Mushroom Duxelles (see page 284) you could use them, or if it's still pheasant back season they'd fit right into these burgers, or chop up some king boletes in the fall.

german-style mushroom potato salad

serves 6

¾ pound small fingerling or red potatoes, quartered

coarse salt

4 slices thick-sliced bacon, cut crosswise into ½-inch pieces

½ pound fresh chanterelles, halved, or lobster mushrooms, torn into bite-size pieces

1 tablespoon olive oil

2 cloves garlic, finely chopped

2 teaspoons brown sugar

2 teaspoons Dijon or brown mustard

3 tablespoons cider vinegar

freshly ground pepper to taste

sliced green onions

Place potatoes in a large pan; cover with water and add 1 teaspoon coarse salt. Bring to a boil; reduce heat and simmer for about 10 minutes or until just tender. Drain well and spoon into a large bowl.

Meanwhile, heat a large skillet over medium-high heat. Cook bacon until crisp; remove bacon with a slotted spoon to drain on paper towels.

Add the mushrooms to the drippings in the skillet. Sauté for about 8 minutes or until tender and beginning to brown. Remove from the skillet to the bowl with the potatoes.

Add the olive oil to the skillet and heat over medium-high heat. Add the garlic, brown sugar, and mustard; cook for 1 minute. Stir in the vinegar and bring to a boil. Remove skillet from heat; season the dressing with salt and pepper. Pour over the potatoes and mushrooms and toss in a handful of green onions and the crisp bacon pieces.

kitchen notes

Potato salad, creamy with mayo or tangy with a vinaigrette, has a standing invitation at all summer picnic tables. A sweet-smoky-vinegary, German-inspired version is a midwestern standard. The inevitable bacon cozies up to the mushrooms as much as to the clean canvas of the potatoes. I look for farmers at open-air markets who mix up both red and yellow potatoes—and even giant sweet potatoes could make a guest appearance. Chop up a cupful to simmer with the fingerlings.

blistered string beans & oyster mushrooms

serves 6

2 tablespoons olive oil

coarse salt and freshly ground pepper to taste

1½ pounds garden green beans, trimmed

½ pound fresh oyster or chanterelle mushrooms, trimmed and sliced

3 cloves garlic, sliced

coarsely chopped fresh herbs, toasted pine nuts, or slivered almonds, if you'd like

Heat a large heavy skillet over high heat until very hot. Pour in oil, then the salt and pepper. Let toast for about 15 seconds, then add the beans and mushrooms. Give the beans and mushrooms a quick stir or shake the pan so they lie in an even layer. Cover the pan and let the vegetables cook for 2 to 3 minutes or until they begin to char.

Uncover and stir the vegetables. Add the garlic; cover pan and continue cooking for about 5 minutes longer or until beans and mushrooms are tender. Serve hot or at room temperature with a handful of herbs or toasted nuts.

kitchen notes

I really like the skinny French green beans (haricots verts), but most often in the summertime I look for baskets of mixed color string beans—green, purple (which magically turn green when cooked), and yellow wax beans. This method of dry-heat cooking forces the natural moisture out of the beans and mushrooms, allowing them to steam until tender without any added liquid. The charring on the beans and around the edges of the mushrooms is visually appetizing, and taste-wise the flavors are concentrated—eliminating any interest I have in adding other seasonings.

herbed mushroom & goat cheese frittata

serves 4 as a main dish or 6 as an appetizer

2 tablespoons olive oil

1 pound mixed fresh wild mushrooms (chanterelle, king bolete, hedgehog), trimmed and thinly sliced

2 cloves garlic, finely chopped

coarse salt and freshly ground pepper to taste

8 large eggs

¾ cup heavy cream

¼ cup (1 ounce) shredded Parmesan cheese

¼ cup coarsely chopped fresh herbs (marjoram, flat-leaf parsley, basil, rosemary), plus extra leaves for garnish

4 ounces soft goat cheese

Heat oven to 375 degrees. Heat oil in a 10-inch ovenproof skillet over medium-high heat. Sauté mushrooms for about 5 minutes or until they release their juices. Reduce heat to medium; stir in garlic and continue cooking about 5 minutes longer, until mushrooms begin to brown. Season with salt and pepper.

Meanwhile, whisk eggs, cream, Parmesan, herbs, ½ teaspoon salt, and a generous grind of pepper together in a medium bowl.

Pour eggs over mushroom mixture; dot goat cheese evenly over top. Cook mixture, stirring and lifting with a rubber spatula, for about 8 minutes or until sides and bottom are set but center is still soft.

Place skillet in the oven; bake for 20 to 25 minutes or until edges puff and brown and the frittata is set. Serve warm, cut into wedges or squares, sprinkled with fresh herbs.

kitchen notes

If your pantry happens to include a basket of forest mushrooms, eggs and mushrooms make for an easy meal or an impromptu snack with a glass of nice red wine. Later in the summer, toss in some freshly picked shaggy manes.

sweet corn fritters with chanterelles & lime crèma

serves 4

½ cup yellow cornmeal

½ cup unbleached all-purpose flour

1¼ teaspoons baking powder

½ teaspoon fine sea salt

2 large eggs

½ cup milk

1¼ cups sour cream, divided

2 cups fresh corn kernels, sliced from the cob (4 medium ears)

⅓ cup sliced green onions

1 tablespoon fresh thyme leaves

olive oil

¾ pound mixed fresh chanterelles, halved, and lobster mushrooms, torn into small pieces

garlic salt and freshly ground pepper to taste

2 medium limes

fresh watercress or peppery nasturtium greens

For the fritter batter, mix cornmeal, flour, baking powder, and ½ teaspoon salt in a large bowl. Whisk in eggs, milk, and ½ cup sour cream until well blended; stir in corn, green onions, and thyme.

Heat 3 tablespoons oil in a large heavy skillet over medium-high heat. Scoop ¼ cup of fritter batter into the oil, flattening a little. Cook for 4 minutes, turning once, or until golden crisp and cooked through. Remove to a plate; keep warm. Repeat with remaining batter.

Heat 2 tablespoons oil in the skillet over medium-high heat. Add mushrooms to the pan; sauté about 8 minutes or until mushrooms are tender and browned. Season with garlic salt and a generous grind of pepper.

Mix remaining ¾ cup sour cream with the grated zest and juice of 1 lime. Cut the second lime into wedges. Serve fritters topped with the mushrooms, a spoonful of the lime crèma, a squeeze of fresh lime juice, and a handful of watercress.

kitchen notes

Grill the corn until it's a little charred before shaving off the kernels if you'd like a smoky edge. Use a sharp chef's blade, slicing down the side of each cob as they lie flat on a cutting board, turning the cob till all the kernels are removed. I've seen fried cakes like these sometimes studded with shredded lobster mushrooms stirred directly into the batter, which would give you weightier cakes that have enough substance to happily be supper.

spiced roasted corn soup with mushroom duxelles

serves 4 to 6

5 medium ears sweet corn, kernels sliced off and cobs reserved

olive oil

1½ teaspoons cumin seed, lightly crushed

½ teaspoon smoked paprika

coarse salt and freshly cracked mixed peppercorns to taste

1 medium red onion, chopped

4 cloves garlic, chopped

1 jalapeño chile, finely chopped

1 teaspoon coriander seed, lightly crushed

4 cups chicken or vegetable broth

1 cup sour cream

1 tablespoon butter

3 tablespoons finely chopped shallot

½ pound mixed fresh wild mushrooms (lobster, oyster, hedgehog), finely chopped

fresh cilantro leaves, slivered red Fresno chile, toasted and salted pumpkin seeds (pepitas)

Heat oven to 425 degrees. Spoon corn kernels onto a parchment-lined rimmed baking sheet. Toss with 2 tablespoons oil, cumin seed, paprika, salt, and pepper; spread out into an even layer. Roast about 15 minutes or until corn is browned in spots.

Heat 1 tablespoon oil in a large soup kettle over medium-high heat. Add the onion, garlic, jalapeño, and coriander. Cook, stirring often, about 4 minutes or until vegetables begin to soften.

Add the corn cobs to kettle, along with the broth and 1 cup water. Bring to a boil; reduce heat and simmer 10 minutes. Discard the cobs. Stir roasted corn into kettle; simmer for 1 minute. Spoon the sour cream into the soup and stir until well blended. Keep soup warm over low heat.

Meanwhile, to make the duxelles, melt butter in a large skillet over medium heat. Cook the shallots for about 3 minutes; add the mushrooms to pan and season with salt and pepper. Cook, stirring often, about 7 minutes or until mushrooms release their juices. Increase heat to medium-high; cook 3 minutes longer or until juices evaporate.

Serve soup in shallow bowls, topped with generous spoonfuls of mushrooms, a scatter of torn cilantro, red chile, and pumpkin seeds.

kitchen notes

Duxelles is a French cooking term defined as a dry purée of mushrooms that is used to flavor soups and stuffings. In the traditional technique, the mushrooms are very finely chopped and sautéed in butter with shallot or onion and garlic and cooked until all the juices in the mushrooms are released and evaporate—leaving an intensely flavored mixture that brings the essence of mushroom to whatever it's stirred into. For this recipe, the mushrooms are not chopped quite as finely and are used as a luscious garnish for the soup.

Using whole cumin and coriander seeds brings a fresh burst of seasoning at each level of the soup. I use a ceramic mortar and pestle to just crush the seeds, and I've also used some flaky smoked salt in a grinder to deepen and round out the broth's flavor.

supper club mushroom (& fish) fry

serves 4

2 cups unbleached all-purpose flour

1 cup cornstarch

1½ teaspoons baking powder

1½ teaspoons coarse sea salt, plus more for seasoning

freshly ground pepper or cayenne to taste

2 eggs

1 (12-ounce) bottle pale ale

peanut or vegetable oil

1½ pounds skinless walleye, northern pike, lake perch, or thin cod fillets, cut into 4 pieces

½ pound fresh lobster or oyster mushrooms, cut into ¼-inch-thick slices

fresh lemon wedges

Creamy Basil Sauce (at right)

Whisk the flour, cornstarch, baking powder, salt, and pepper together in a large bowl. Stir in the eggs and ale until batter is smooth. Cover and chill while the oil is heating up.

Pour enough oil into a large Dutch oven to bring the level to 2 inches. Turn the heat to medium; bring the temperature to 375 degrees (use a thermometer or drop a bit of batter in to see if it sizzles).

Have paper towel–lined trays ready. Dry the fish well and season with more salt and pepper. Dip 1 fish fillet at a time into the batter. When the oil is hot, shake any excess batter from fish and lower it into the hot oil. Cook about 5 minutes or until golden brown; drain on tray. Adjust heat to keep the oil hot and repeat with the rest of the fish.

Cover the fish and keep it warm. Dip the mushrooms in the batter a batch at a time, dropping them into the oil. Cook 3 to 4 minutes or until golden. Repeat until all the mushrooms are fried; drain well on tray.

Serve the fish with the crisp mushrooms, with lemon wedges, and with a dish of basil sauce for dipping.

Creamy Basil Sauce: Mix ¾ cup plain Greek yogurt, ½ cup sour cream, ½ teaspoon garlic salt or to taste, ½ teaspoon grated lemon zest, 1 to 2 tablespoons fresh lemon juice, and ¼ cup chopped fresh basil until well blended.

kitchen notes
Go full mushroom fry if your fishing luck goes bust. Some days you just can't have both.

smoked coriander-brined stream trout with chanterelles

serves 6 to 8

4 fresh whole brook trout (about 3 pounds total), dressed

8 cups water

¾ cup packed brown sugar

½ cup coarse salt, plus more for seasoning

3 teaspoons coriander seed, lightly crushed, divided

1 teaspoon red pepper flakes

2 tablespoons olive oil

1 pound fresh chanterelle mushrooms, trimmed and halved

freshly ground pepper to taste

toasted slices crusty bread or crispbreads

fresh goat cheese or other local cheeses

torn fresh cilantro leaves

Place fish in a large glass baking dish or jumbo resealable plastic bag. Mix the water, brown sugar, ½ cup salt, 2 teaspoons coriander, and red pepper flakes until the sugar dissolves. Pour the brine over the fish; cover the dish or seal the bag. Refrigerate for a few hours.

Drain and rinse the fish. Follow the directions for your smoker, using a mild wood like apple, oak, or alder. Smaller trout can be done within an hour, but the flavor is best if they smoke for up to 4 hours at a temperature of about 225 degrees.

When the trout are nearly ready, heat the oil in a large skillet over medium-high heat. Add the mushrooms and season them with salt, pepper, and the remaining 1 teaspoon coriander. Sauté for about 8 minutes or until they release their juices and begin to brown.

Spread the toasted bread with cheese and top with flaked smoked trout and mushrooms, sprinkled with cilantro.

kitchen notes

I've never had great luck growing cilantro in my yard; it bolts while I'm looking elsewhere, or our neighborhood woodchucks are taken with chewing down the stalks. I settle instead for harvesting the flowering seed heads, which are the source of coriander seed. I dry them to use in my own spice blends, and they're wonderful in a brining liquid.

A stash of this smoked trout is reason for a party, especially if you also have wild mushrooms on hand. But if cocktail dining doesn't work for you, make a big pot of creamy pasta studded with the smoked fish and mushrooms.

prairie wheat berry salad with roasted mushrooms & chioggia beets

serves 4

½ cup uncooked wheat berries, toasted in a dry skillet if you'd like

coarse salt

6 ounces fresh small to medium chanterelle mushrooms, halved

3 small Chioggia or golden beets, scrubbed and cut into wedges (save the greens if they aren't too wilted to toss into the salad)

2 tablespoons olive oil

freshly ground pepper to taste

⅓ cup white wine vinegar

2 tablespoons finely chopped shallot

2 tablespoons honey

¼ cup hazelnut or walnut oil

1 (15-ounce) can garbanzo beans, rinsed and drained

4 cups fresh baby arugula

2 cups fresh lemon balm leaves or a combination of other favorite herbs

Heat oven to 425 degrees. Place wheat berries in a medium saucepan; pour in 3 cups water and ½ teaspoon salt. Bring to a boil; reduce heat and simmer for 40 minutes or just until barely tender (a little bite is good).

Meanwhile, line a large rimmed baking sheet with parchment. Toss the mushrooms and beets with olive oil; season with salt and pepper. Arrange in a single layer on the baking sheet. Roast for about 20 minutes or until tender and mushrooms start to brown.

Whisk the vinegar, shallot, and honey together in a small bowl; whisk in the nut oil until the vinaigrette thickens slightly and season with salt and pepper.

When the wheat berries are done, drain them well and spoon into a medium bowl. Add the garbanzo beans and a few spoonfuls of the dressing; toss well. Arrange the arugula and herbs on large plates. Spoon the wheat berry mixture over the greens and the mushrooms and beets alongside. Spoon the rest of the dressing over the salads.

kitchen notes

In the summertime when fresh herbs are spilling over farmers' market tables, I can't resist buying huge bouquets of cilantro with the roots still attached, lavender-tinged Thai basil, sprays of fragrant dill, and a world of mints, oregano, and sage. It may seem impossible to use them up, but making them a part of your salad greens lineup is a natural solution. The large lemon balm leaves tossed into this earthy salad offer up a burst of a slightly minty, slightly lemony freshness. I've made this pretty salad as a meal starter, teamed with some good aged cheese and a chunk of smoked salmon for a dinner party. Or it can just be the stuff of a small-plate supper.

dog days bounty

chanterelle & corn calabacitas with spicy grilled shrimp

serves 4

2 tablespoons olive oil

1 tablespoon butter

6 cloves garlic, thinly sliced

½ pound fresh chanterelle and/or oyster mushrooms, torn or sliced

5 green onions, sliced

2–3 medium ears sweet corn, kernels sliced from cobs

1 small zucchini, chopped

1 red Fresno chile, finely chopped

coarse salt and freshly ground pepper

½ cup mixed color cherry tomatoes, halved

torn fresh Mexican oregano leaves to taste

1 pound (16–20 count) large uncooked, peeled, tail-on shrimp

2 teaspoons Tajín or Cajun blackened fish seasoning

fresh lime wedges

Heat the oil and butter in a large deep skillet over medium-high heat. Add the garlic and mushrooms; sauté about 5 minutes or until mushrooms begin to brown around the edges and garlic is golden. Add the onions, corn, zucchini, and red chile. Season with salt and pepper; sauté another 6 to 8 minutes or until everything is tender. Toss in the tomatoes and oregano; cook another 2 minutes.

Meanwhile, heat a stovetop grill or heavy grill pan over high heat. Toss the shrimp with the spicy seasoning. Thread onto bamboo skewers. Lightly oil the stovetop grill grids or pan, then cook the shrimp just until no longer translucent in the center. Spoon the mushroom-corn mixture onto plates. Serve topped with the shrimp and a squeeze of lime.

kitchen notes

There are so many good, spicy seasoning blends available straight off the shelf, but one of my favorites is Tajín from Mexico. It's hard to discern the exact ingredients, but it's clear that ground red chile is a central player, partnered with salt and lime. It has lots of flavor and just a little kick and is easy to find at any Hispanic market. If you'd like more heat than the dry seasoning and Fresno chile add, shake in some of the unending variety of hot pepper sauces available these days. The buttery-rich edge the mushrooms give to the corn sauté is a good counterpoint to the tender, spicy shrimp, which you could just quickly cook in the same hot skillet after the vegetables are done, if making and grilling skewers is one step too many.

grilled puffball bruschetta

serves 4

8 slices (about ¼ pound, cut into ¾-inch-thick slices) fresh giant puffball mushroom

olive oil

coarse salt, freshly ground pepper, and crushed red pepper flakes to taste

2 large Brandywine or Cherokee purple tomatoes or 3 medium plum tomatoes, chopped

2 tomatillos, husked, rinsed, and chopped

2 cloves garlic, finely chopped

fresh basil leaves, torn

aged dark or white balsamic vinegar

Heat the grill to medium-high. Brush both sides of each mushroom slice with oil. Season with salt and pepper. Place the slices on the grill; cook for 5 to 6 minutes, turning once, until golden brown (they'll have distinct grill marks) and tender inside.

Transfer the slices to a serving platter. Mix the tomatoes, tomatillos, garlic, and a nice splash of olive oil. Season with salt and pepper. Spoon the tomatoes on top of each mushroom slice and sprinkle on fresh basil and a drizzle of balsamic vinegar.

kitchen notes

Depending on the size of the puffballs you find, you may want to peel off the somewhat leathery outer skin of each slice—very easy to do with just a little nick on one edge with a paring knife. The texture of a good puffball should be firm and sort of spongy-dense, with a bright white interior. They make a perfect canvas for boldly flavored toppings, though the classic juicy summer-ripe tomato (especially some of the meatier heirloom varieties) and garlic combo is always my go-to during the torrent of peak tomatoes. These bruschetta are a knife-and-fork meal starter; the mushrooms are smoky and tender after grilling, too soft to pick up and eat out of hand.

I'm a huge believer in tailoring food to personal tastes, so take this straightforward template for bruschetta-style snacks and set out small dishes of delicious DIY toppings.

Olive tapenade

Chopped pickled vegetables

Sliced sweet cherry tomatoes

Other herbs, like fresh mint or oregano

Crumbly goat cheese

Thinly sliced cured or smoked meats—salami, prosciutto, soppressata, speck

a vegetarian bbq

serves 4

1¼ pounds fresh lobster or chicken of the woods mushrooms, trimmed and rinsed

4 medium ears sweet corn, in the husk

¾ cup (6 ounces) softened butter (or ¾ cup Compound Wild Mushroom Herb Butter, see page 289)

½ cup finely chopped summer herbs (parsley, basil, thyme, and/or rosemary)

2 cloves garlic, finely chopped

coarse salt and freshly ground pepper to taste

ground chipotle powder or hot smoked paprika

Heat the grill to medium-high. If you have lobster mushrooms, tear them into large chunks; cut chicken of the woods into 1-inch-thick slices. Bring a large pot of salted water to a boil; drop the mushrooms into the boiling water, poaching them for about 3 minutes. Drain well and lay them out on a tray.

Meanwhile, pull the husks down from the corn and remove the corn silk. Whisk the butter, herbs, and garlic together until well blended. Brush some over the mushrooms and the corn; season with salt and pepper.

Place the mushrooms and corn on the grill; cover and cook for about 8 minutes, turning once, or until tender and charred. Brush occasionally with more of the flavored butter.

Sprinkle everything with a little smoky chipotle powder or paprika. Serve with any remaining butter.

kitchen notes
The meatiness of lobster or chicken of the woods makes them perfect for grilling, low and slow over indirect heat, until they are as smoky and delicious as a good steak. The use of the tag "bbq" for barbecue usually annoys me, but the irreverent spelling fits perfectly as a big mushroom stands in for other more traditional center-of-the-plate candidates.

mushroom, walnut & lentil burgers with pickled onions

serves 8

1 medium red onion

¾ cup seasoned rice vinegar

½ teaspoon crushed red pepper flakes

1 cup coarsely chopped walnuts

olive oil

½ pound fresh chanterelle, oyster, or hedgehog mushrooms, roughly chopped (3 cups)

1 cup cooked lentils

¼ cup fresh dill sprigs

2 tablespoons cold butter, cut into pieces

1 egg, lightly beaten

2 cups cooked freekeh, bulgur, quinoa, or brown rice

1 cup uncooked old-fashioned oats, divided

4 cloves garlic, crushed in a garlic press (or 2 teaspoons garlic paste)

2 tablespoons mayonnaise

1 tablespoon Worcestershire sauce

2½ teaspoons coarse salt

freshly ground pepper to taste

toasted whole-grain buns

crumbled local blue cheese

Thinly slice red onion, finely chopping part of it to make ¼ cup. Put the chopped onion into a large bowl; place the remaining sliced onion in a medium bowl and stir in seasoned rice vinegar and red pepper flakes. Cover and refrigerate.

Toast the walnuts in a large heavy skillet over medium-high heat until fragrant. Pour them into a food processor fit with the metal blade.

Heat 1 tablespoon oil in the skillet; sauté the mushrooms for about 6 minutes or until their juices are released and they are just tender. Scrape them into the food processor, along with the lentils, dill, and butter. Pulse the blade until all the ingredients are well chopped (not puréed). Scrape into the bowl with the chopped red onion.

Stir in the egg, freekeh, ½ cup oats, garlic, mayonnaise, Worcestershire, salt, and pepper until the mixture is well blended. Cover and chill mixture for 30 minutes. Shape into 8 thick patties, using the remaining ½ cup oats to help form them.

Heat a cast-iron or nonstick skillet over medium-high heat. Add 2 tablespoons oil and cook the patties in batches for about 8 minutes, turning once, or until browned and crisp. Serve on toasted buns with pickled red onions and blue cheese.

kitchen notes
Mushrooms bring a full savoriness to meatless burgers. These are moist and tender, so pan-grilling them in a heavy skillet or sliding them onto a griddle on a smoky grill will ensure they don't fall apart during cooking. I like to use a mixture of mushrooms, though I usually stick with faster-cooking varieties like chanterelles, oysters, or hedgehogs. This time of the summer you'll have good options, maybe even a basket of king boletes. For the lentils and grains, I'll often short-cut with pouches of precooked ingredients. I've found very nice cooked black beluga lentils and all sorts of interesting grain mixes right off the shelf.

fancy farmhouse toasts

serves 4

½ pound mixed fresh wild mushrooms (chanterelle, oyster, hedgehog, and/or king bolete), trimmed and halved or sliced

1 cup cherry tomatoes

olive oil

coarse salt and freshly ground pepper to taste

4 ounces soft goat cheese

1 small lemon, zested and juiced

1 teaspoon finely chopped fresh thyme leaves

2 large cloves garlic, thinly sliced

4 large (½-inch-thick) slices crusty bread (country-style sourdough, potato, or rye bread), lightly toasted

1 cup tiny arugula or other spicy microgreens

crushed red pepper flakes to taste

Heat oven to 425 degrees. Line a large rimmed baking sheet with parchment. Toss the mushrooms and tomatoes with 1 tablespoon oil. Season with salt and pepper. Spread out on the baking sheet; roast for about 15 minutes or until the mushrooms are tender and tomatoes begin to burst.

Meanwhile, mix goat cheese, lemon zest and juice, thyme, and ground pepper in a small bowl.

Heat 2 tablespoons oil in a small skillet over medium-high heat. Add garlic; cook for about 1 minute or until golden. Remove garlic and drain on paper toweling; reserve oil.

Spread toast with the goat cheese mixture; top with the warm mushrooms and tomatoes and garlic slices. Drizzle with garlic oil; top with microgreens and red pepper flakes.

kitchen notes

Toast, tartines, crostini, smørbrød . . . simply open-face sandwiches by lots of names. There's a Scandinavian tradition to make casual sandwiches from just about any ingredient. Toss in whatever bits of mushrooms you've got for a delicious roasted topping for crunchy toasts. Look for the best bread you can find—I like either airy ciabatta or dense rye—and be sure to get some good browning around the edges before topping it. Mine the late-summer harvest for other roasting partners for the savory mushrooms, like sliced sweet bell peppers or cubed eggplant. A forkful of smoked fish or thin shards of aged cheese would be nice finishes.

sautéed mushroom lasagna stacks

serves 4

8 lasagna noodles, broken in half

1 cup packed fresh basil leaves, plus more for garnish

½ cup olive oil

coarse salt

¾ cup ricotta cheese

¾ cup (3 ounces) finely shredded asiago cheese (with rosemary if you'd like), divided

2 cloves garlic, finely chopped

½ pound mixed fresh wild mushrooms (hedgehog, black trumpet, and/or chanterelle), trimmed and sliced

2 cups mixed color cherry tomatoes, halved

freshly ground pepper to taste

1 medium zucchini, halved lengthwise and sliced crosswise, or 2–3 baby zucchini, sliced

1 medium yellow summer squash, halved lengthwise and sliced crosswise

Cook noodles according to package directions; rinse and drain (return to pot with a little warm water to keep noodles from sticking together). While the noodles are cooking, set the basil leaves in a strainer and dip into the hot pasta water; blanch for 1 minute. Rinse with cold water; drain well and squeeze dry in a paper towel. Place in a blender or food processor with the oil and ⅛ teaspoon salt and process until puréed. Pour the basil oil into a squeeze bottle.

Mix the ricotta and 3 tablespoons asiago cheese in a small bowl; set aside.

Heat 1 tablespoon basil oil in a large skillet over medium-high heat. Add the garlic; sauté for 1 minute. Add the firmer mushrooms (hedgehogs and/or chanterelles) to skillet. Cook and stir for 6 minutes. Stir in the black trumpets if using and continue cooking for about 3 minutes longer or until all the mushrooms are tender and browned. Scrape into a bowl.

Heat 1 tablespoon basil oil in the skillet over medium-high heat. Add the tomatoes; season with salt and pepper. Cook and stir about 3 minutes or until they soften and start breaking apart. Transfer to a second bowl. Heat 1 tablespoon basil oil in the skillet; stir in the zucchini and squash and season with salt and pepper. Sauté about 6 minutes or until squash is tender and browned. Scrape into the bowl with the tomatoes.

To assemble the lasagna, spoon some mushrooms and vegetables onto 4 large plates. Top with a piece of noodle, small spoonfuls of the ricotta mixture, and more mushrooms and vegetables. Repeat layering twice, ending with a spoonful of mushrooms and the remaining asiago cheese. Garnish with fresh basil leaves and another drizzle of basil oil. Refrigerate any leftover basil oil for up to 1 week.

kitchen notes

In the summer heat these layered stacks of pasta are a fresher take on a cool-weather baked lasagna—and really show off the mushrooms. Blending the black trumpets with hedgehogs or chanterelles offers a nice balance of color and rounds out the flavor.

chargrilled triple mushroom pizza

serves 12

olive oil

1 small red onion, sliced

1¼ pounds mixed fresh wild mushrooms (hedgehog, lobster, black trumpet)

coarse salt and freshly ground pepper to taste

1–2 tablespoons finely chopped fresh rosemary leaves

yellow cornmeal

1½ pounds whole-grain pizza dough (purchased or homemade), divided in half

½ cup Roasted Garlic Paste (at right) or purchased garlic sauce

4 ounces goat cheese, crumbled

Heat 1 tablespoon oil in a large skillet over medium-high heat. Add the onion; sauté for 5 minutes or until tender and beginning to char a bit around the edges. Scrape into a bowl.

Heat 2 tablespoons oil in the skillet. Add the hedgehog and lobster mushrooms first; sauté for 5 to 6 minutes. Add the black trumpets and cook for about 3 minutes longer or until tender. Season with salt, pepper, and the rosemary. Remove skillet from heat and cover with foil or a lid.

Meanwhile, heat a grill to medium-low. Sprinkle 2 large flat baking sheets with cornmeal. Stretch and roll out 1 ball of pizza dough into a 12-inch round (it's fine if it's an irregular shape; let the dough rest for a few minutes if it's bouncing back); place on baking sheet. Repeat with the second ball of dough.

Lightly grease the grill rack. Slide both dough rounds directly onto the grill. Cook for about 4 minutes or until the bottom of crusts is golden brown. Turn over the crust using a baking sheet, pizza peel, or wide spatula.

Quickly spread each crust with ¼ cup garlic paste or sauce; top with onions and mushrooms. Dot with goat cheese. Cover grill and cook for 3 to 5 minutes longer or until cheese is softened and the crusts are a bit charred and a deep golden brown.

Roasted Garlic Paste: Heat oven to 375 degrees. Slice off and discard the top third of 2 to 3 heads of garlic. Place them on a large square of foil; drizzle with ⅓ cup olive oil and season with salt and pepper. Fold the foil up and over the garlic heads; fold to seal well. Bake for 45 minutes; open up the foil packet. Continue baking for about 15 minutes longer or until the cloves begin to squeeze out of their papery skin. Let the garlic heads cool, then squeeze the soft cloves into a bowl. Use a fork to mash them with the oil left in the foil packet to make a spreadable paste, then stir in 1 tablespoon red wine vinegar or fresh lemon juice and a few grinds of salt and pepper. Double the number of garlic heads to have some of this paste on hand for other dishes.

kitchen notes

To boost the smoky undertones of a grilled pizza, toss in some water-soaked wood chips and allow them to smolder for a

(Continued next page)

while before sliding the dough onto the grill. If you have a few extra minutes, consider grilling or smoking the mushrooms to top each crust.

I've become quite preoccupied by "new" varieties of heirloom wheats and flours that seem to be better for some folks who are gluten sensitive, though I'm still more about baking with whole-grain flours in general. I'm a dedicated user of easily accessible unbleached bread flours (higher protein than an all-purpose or pastry flour). But when it comes to pizza, I'm all for making it easy: you can actually order pizza dough from some of the milling companies that specialize in heirloom wheat, or I've bought dough from favorite local bakeries that feature whole-grain breads.

· · · · ·

mushroom XO sauce with roasted cauliflower steaks

serves 4

½ pound fresh king bolete mushrooms, trimmed and finely chopped

1 tablespoon toasted sesame oil

1 teaspoon mushroom soy sauce or tamari

1 tablespoon fermented black beans, rinsed and mashed

1 tablespoon roasted garlic–seasoned rice vinegar

2 teaspoons Asian hot pepper sauce

¼ cup water

1 large head cauliflower, sliced vertically into 4 slabs

2 tablespoons peanut oil

coarse salt and freshly ground pepper to taste

Heat oven to 450 degrees. Line a large rimmed baking sheet with parchment. Toss the mushrooms with the sesame oil; spread in an even layer on the baking sheet. Roast for 10 to 12 minutes, stirring occasionally, until the mushrooms have released their juices and are golden brown. Scrape them into a bowl (keep the parchment on the baking pan). Stir in the soy, black beans, vinegar, hot pepper sauce, and water until well blended; cover and set aside.

Lay out the cauliflower on the baking sheet; drizzle with the peanut oil and season with salt and pepper. Roast for about 35 minutes, turning once, or until very tender and golden brown. Serve cauliflower topped with spoonfuls of the XO sauce.

kitchen notes
I first learned about XO sauce in San Francisco. This souped-up Chinese condiment is filled with expensive, deeply rich, and intense ingredients liked smoked scallops and premium Chinese ham—thus the XO moniker that refers to a super-pricey Cognac, automatically conferring an exclusiveness in both cost and flavor. But taken to its most common denominator, an XO sauce is all about salty, smoky, spicy-sweet umami—which wild mushrooms have in spades. Just a spoonful is enough to take the most elegantly simple vegetable to new places. Keep a jarful in the fridge for up to a few weeks.

COW burgers with grilled onions & swiss

serves 4

2 eggs, lightly beaten

olive oil

¾ cup panko bread crumbs

1 teaspoon barbecue seasoning spice blend

coarse salt and freshly ground pepper to taste

4 pieces fresh chicken of the woods mushroom, about ½-inch thick (about the size of a small chicken breast fillet; about 3 ounces each)

4 slices (4 ounces) Swiss cheese

2 medium red or yellow onions, sliced

fresh thyme leaves to taste

4 whole-grain kaiser or onion rolls, split and toasted

Mix eggs and 1 tablespoon oil in a shallow dish. Stir together the bread crumbs, barbecue seasoning, salt, and pepper in a second shallow dish.

Dip a mushroom slice in the eggs, then dredge it in the bread crumbs. Repeat with the rest of the mushrooms.

Heat 2 tablespoons oil in a large heavy skillet over medium-high heat. Cook the mushrooms, in batches if needed, for 10 to 15 minutes or until crisp and golden, turning once. Remove to a platter and top with a slice of cheese. Tent the mushrooms with foil and let stand for 10 minutes (the cheese will melt) while you cook the onions.

Heat 2 tablespoons oil in the skillet. Add the onions; season with salt and pepper. Sauté for about 6 minutes or until tender and a bit charred and browned; stir in some thyme. Sandwich the mushrooms in the toasted rolls, topped with onions.

kitchen notes

I'm sorry for the bad play on words, but when Michael told me that some hunters use the acronym *COW* for chicken of the woods mushrooms, I couldn't resist. For a little more zip, smear the mushroom cutlets with a spoonful of spicy mustard before dipping them in bread crumbs mixed with a little grated aged cheese, then bake them at 425 degrees for about 20 minutes or until the mushrooms are tender inside with a crispy exterior. Serve them hot with a side of sauerkraut and freshly grated horseradish.

mushroom-stuffed zucchini boats

serves 4 to 8

4 medium zucchini, trimmed

2 tablespoons butter, divided

1 tablespoon olive oil

2 cloves garlic, finely chopped

½ pound fresh wild mushrooms (oyster, hedgehog, king bolete), chopped

¾ cup coarse fresh whole-grain bread crumbs

¼ cup chopped walnuts

2 large eggs, lightly beaten

½ cup chopped plum tomato

¾ cup freshly grated Parmesan cheese, divided

coarse salt and freshly ground pepper to taste

chopped or torn fresh oregano, rosemary, and/or basil to taste

Heat oven to 375 degrees. Bring a large kettle of water to a boil; add zucchini. Cook for about 10 minutes or until tender. Drain well; slice in half lengthwise. Scoop out centers with a spoon and coarsely chop, then place in a medium bowl. Arrange zucchini halves on a large parchment-lined rimmed baking sheet.

Meanwhile, heat 1 tablespoon butter and the oil in a large skillet over medium-high heat. Add garlic and mushrooms; sauté about 6 minutes or until the mushrooms release their juices and begin to brown. Scrape into the bowl with the zucchini centers.

Melt remaining 1 tablespoon butter in skillet; add bread crumbs and walnuts. Cook and stir about 4 minutes or until browned and toasted. Add to the mushroom-zucchini mixture.

Stir eggs, tomato, and ¼ cup cheese into the bowl; season with salt and pepper. Lightly salt inside each zucchini (drain any accumulated liquid), then spoon in the filling; sprinkle with remaining ½ cup cheese.

Bake 20 to 25 minutes or until golden brown. Serve hot or at room temperature sprinkled with herbs.

kitchen notes

A little putzy, this dish is adapted from my mother's stuffed zucchini from when I was a kid. In the late summer, as we're overrun with zucchini and summer squash, it's an old-fashioned way to get to yet one more appealing side dish or even a vegetarian main. My mom would often use ground beef in her stuffing, but I like the lighter savoriness of the mushrooms.

swedish meatballs with creamy chanterelle gravy

serves 6 as a main dish or 10 as an appetizer (24 meatballs)

3 slices whole-grain bread, torn into pieces (about 1½ cups)

½ cup milk

olive oil

¾ cup finely chopped onion

1½ pounds ground elk, venison, or a combination of lean beef and pork

1 large egg, lightly beaten

1 clove garlic, finely chopped

coarse salt and freshly ground pepper

¼ teaspoon ground nutmeg

¼ teaspoon ground allspice

¼ teaspoon ground ginger

3 tablespoons butter, divided

½ pound fresh chanterelle mushrooms, trimmed and thickly sliced

1 tablespoon unbleached all-purpose flour

1 cup mushroom (see page 292) or chicken stock

¼ cup heavy cream

chopped fresh dill and parsley

sweetened lingonberry sauce

Mix bread pieces and milk in a small bowl. Let soak for about 5 minutes. Meanwhile, heat 1 tablespoon oil in a large deep skillet over medium-high heat. Sauté onion 3 to 4 minutes or until nearly tender. Scrape into a large bowl.

Stir the softened bread into the onions, then add the ground meat, egg, garlic, 1½ teaspoons salt, ½ teaspoon pepper and spices. Mix gently until all the ingredients are very well blended. Moisten your hands in cool water and roll the meat mixture into 1-inch balls, laying them out on a tray.

Heat 1 tablespoon oil and 2 tablespoons butter in the large skillet over medium heat. Add meatballs, cooking half of them at a time, for about 4 minutes or until well browned. Drain them on a paper towel–lined tray.

Add remaining 1 tablespoon butter to skillet. Add mushrooms; season with salt and pepper. Sauté for about 8 minutes, until their juices are released and they begin to brown. Sprinkle with flour. Continue cooking, stirring constantly, for 1 minute. Stir in stock and cream; bring to a boil. Return meatballs to pan and reduce heat to medium. Simmer the meatballs and sauce, shaking the pan occasionally, for about 10 minutes or until gravy is thickened and meatballs are cooked through.

Serve meatballs with the gravy, sprinkled with herbs and with a dish of lingonberry sauce on the side.

kitchen notes

Be ready to give these meatballs a little TLC: they're moist and not too compact, so use a light hand when you brown them in the skillet. It's worth the extra care, especially if you use lean game meat. I like finding small imported jars of lingonberry (Arctic cranberry) sauce to balance the richness of the overall dish, but a tart spiced cranberry relish would be a good substitute.

grilled lamb chops with chanterelles & wild blueberry chutney

serves 4 to 6

olive oil

½ pound fresh small (button) chanterelle mushrooms, trimmed

½ cup wild or small domestic blueberries

1 cup white wine vinegar

¼ cup water

2 tablespoons sugar

1 small clove garlic, finely chopped

coarse salt

dash red pepper flakes

fresh thyme, oregano, and/or mint (with some flowering tops if you have any)

2 (8-rib, about 1½ pounds each) Frenched racks of lamb, cut into chops

freshly ground pepper to taste

Heat 1 tablespoon oil a large skillet over medium-high heat. Add the mushrooms, in batches, and cook for about 6 minutes, until they release their juices. Remove to a medium glass or ceramic bowl and stir in blueberries.

Add the vinegar, water, sugar, garlic, 1 teaspoon salt, red pepper flakes, and some sprigs of fresh herbs to the skillet; bring to a boil. Reduce heat and simmer for 5 minutes. Pour hot liquid over the mushrooms and blueberries. Cover and let stand for at least 1 hour (or refrigerate overnight).

Meanwhile, heat grill to medium-high heat. Lightly brush the lamb with oil and season with salt and pepper. Grill chops for about 8 minutes, turning once, for medium-rare.

Serve the lamb with slightly drained spoonfuls of the chanterelle-blueberry chutney, sprinkled with flowering herbs.

kitchen notes

Wild blueberries are ripening in the north woods at the same time chanterelles are popping up all over the forest floor. The contrasting colors and flavors of the midnight-purple berries with the almost neon-yellow of the mushrooms are striking; lightly pickled in a practically-instant savory-sweet chutney, they add a tangy edge to richly grilled meats. Use the smallest of the mushrooms you harvest so you can leave them whole.

Lamb, especially grilled chops, is a favorite for me, but any bone-in chop would be equally delicious: try elk, venison, or pork. Recently I ran across a modern Finnish recipe for thinly sliced salted fillet of lamb with lots of delicate summer herbs and pickled tiny chanterelles; the flavors just work.

The chanterelle-berry chutney—a condiment meant to be eaten immediately rather than preserved like a pickle—can be refrigerated for up to a week. If you have a chanterelle windfall, double the recipe and serve it as part of a snack platter with some good local cheeses and crisp flatbreads.

west side tacos with grilled mushrooms, corn & rajas de poblano

serves 4

1 large poblano chile

2 medium ears sweet corn, husked

1 tablespoon cumin seed

2 tablespoons plus 1 teaspoon olive oil

½ pound fresh wild oyster, black trumpet, and/or chanterelle mushrooms, trimmed and sliced or torn into small pieces

coarse salt and freshly ground pepper to taste

8 (6-inch) white or yellow corn tortillas, lightly grilled

1 cup cooked black or pinto beans

1 avocado, peeled and chopped

6 small radishes, sliced

2 green onions, sliced

1 cup (4 ounces) crumbled Cotija cheese

fresh lime wedges, torn fresh cilantro leaves, and hot pepper sauce to taste

Roast the poblano over an open gas flame, under the broiler, or on the grill until most of the skin is blackened. Place in a small paper bag; set aside to steam for about 10 minutes. Peel away the charred waxy skin with a paring knife; discard stem and seeds. Slice the chile into strips and put into a bowl.

Roast the corn the same way you roasted the chile, but just until lightly charred. Slice the kernels off the cobs and add to the poblano strips.

Lightly toast cumin in a small dry skillet over medium heat, just until fragrant. Pour seeds into a mortar and pestle or onto a cutting board. Add a teaspoon of oil; grind seeds to a coarse paste with the pestle or edge of a knife blade. Add 2 tablespoons oil to paste.

Heat a heavy skillet over medium-high heat. Add the cumin-oil paste, stirring constantly for 1 minute. Add the mushrooms; sauté for about 8 minutes or until they release their juices and are crispy around the edges. Season with salt and pepper.

Stir the poblano strips and corn kernels into the skillet; cook for about 1 minute or until heated through.

Spoon mushroom-vegetable mixture into the warm tortillas. Top with a spoonful of beans, avocado, radish, onions, and cheese as you like. Serve lime, cilantro, and hot pepper sauce alongside.

kitchen notes

Mexican street-style tacos are a great vehicle for highlighting grilled wild mushrooms, roasted hot chiles, and summery corn. The West Side of St. Paul, Minnesota, is home to a vibrant Hispanic community that continues to expand and influence food styles in the region. In the summer, one of my favorite markets there sells smoky ears of corn (*elote*) dripping with Mexican crema and mayo and showered with coarsely chopped fresh cilantro, ground red chile, and Cotija cheese—all made on a big grill at the edge of the parking lot.

Rajas are roasted strips of poblano chile, which have some heat but aren't incendiary in the world of chiles. If you'd like more heat, finely chop a fresno or serrano chile and stir it into some coarsely mashed avocado with lime juice and torn cilantro—guacamole in a moment.

sautéed greens & lion's mane with sultanas & pine nuts

serves 4

olive oil

½ pound fresh lion's mane mushrooms, rinsed and torn into bite-size pieces

4 cloves garlic, finely chopped

coarse salt and freshly ground pepper to taste

1 bunch broccoli rabe (rapini), trimmed and chopped

1 large bunch red or rainbow Swiss chard or red kale, leafy parts torn and stems chopped

½ cup chopped onion

⅓ cup golden raisins

¼ cup white wine or apple cider

¼ cup pine nuts, toasted

1 cup red grapes, halved

white balsamic vinegar

Heat 2 tablespoons oil in a large heavy skillet over medium-high heat. Add mushrooms and half of the garlic; season with salt and pepper. Sauté for about 8 minutes or until the mushrooms are crispy and golden brown. Scrape into a bowl.

Heat 2 tablespoons oil in the skillet. Add the second half of the garlic, the stems of the broccoli rabe and the chard, and the onion. Sauté for 5 minutes or until softened. Add the broccoli rabe tops, the leafy chard, the raisins, and the wine. Cover the pan; reduce heat to medium and let the mixture steam for about 5 minutes. Uncover and continue cooking until the vegetables are tender. Season with salt and pepper.

Stir mushrooms into greens. Serve warm salad garnished with the pine nuts, grapes, and a splash of vinegar.

kitchen notes

Sultanas are a specific type of white grape and have a sweeter tang than dark raisins—and I like how they almost glow when mixed in with the darker greens. Beet greens could be swapped for the chard or kale, but definitely use the broccoli rabe. Its slight bitterness just seems to work with lion's mane, especially if the mushrooms have a nice golden-brown finish. This style of greens is a favorite for topping pizzas or flatbreads in many parts of the Mediterranean.

autumnal equinox

apple & honey–glazed duck with roasted potatoes & mushrooms

serves 4

2 whole skin-on wild ducks (about 3 pounds total)

flaked smoked salt and freshly ground pepper to taste

½ cup crabapple or apple jelly

¼ cup floral honey

hot pepper flakes to taste

1 pound small red potatoes, quartered

½ pound fresh lobster and/or king bolete mushrooms, trimmed and sliced

olive oil

2 heads garlic, cut in half crosswise

fresh thyme sprigs and leaves

Heat oven to 425 degrees. Adjust oven racks so the ducks can be placed in the center of the oven and the potatoes and mushrooms can slide in on the rack below. Line 2 rimmed baking sheets with parchment.

Season the ducks inside and out with salt and pepper; arrange on a baking sheet. Mix the jelly, honey, and hot pepper flakes together until smooth.

Toss the potatoes and mushrooms with 2 tablespoons oil; season with salt and pepper. Arrange on the second baking sheet. Place the garlic head halves on the pan; drizzle with 1 tablespoon oil.

Place the ducks and potato-mushroom mixture in the oven; roast for 15 minutes. Reduce heat to 350 degrees. Brush the ducks generously with the jelly-honey mixture; stir the potatoes and mushrooms.

Continue roasting for 20 to 30 minutes, brushing the ducks a few more times with the glaze, until the ducks are golden brown and no longer pink near the bone. The potatoes and mushrooms should all be browned and crisp.

Cut the birds in half to serve with the potatoes, mushrooms, and garlic. Sprinkle with fresh thyme leaves.

kitchen notes

Wild ducks are much leaner than their barnyard cousins, so a hot oven will crisp them up in just over half an hour. Mallards are the birds of the hour here, most likely foraging for their supper out in fields of grain versus fishing in their ponds. Some autumn crabapple jelly and local honey nicely complement the rich meat—and the sweetly savory pan juices are wonderful with the roasted potatoes and mushrooms. Squeeze out the tender garlic cloves to smash with your fork with each bite. This might be the time to add some braised sweet-sour red cabbage to the menu.

autumn mushroom & butternut tart

serves 6

1¾ cups unbleached all-purpose flour

2¼ cups (9 ounces) shredded white cheddar or Swiss cheese, divided

½ teaspoon fine salt

½ cup (4 ounces) cold butter, cut into chunks

2 egg yolks

3 tablespoons ice water

7–8 (½-inch-thick) slices (about ½ pound) peeled butternut squash or unpeeled delicata squash

olive oil

coarse salt and freshly ground pepper to taste

freshly grated nutmeg and toasted ground cumin to taste

¾ pound mixed fresh wild mushrooms (chanterelles, hen of the woods, king boletes, or black trumpets), trimmed and sliced

fresh sage leaves and sliced green onions, if you'd like

Heat oven to 450 degrees. To make the pastry crust, place the flour, 1 cup cheese, and salt in the bowl of a food processor fit with the metal blade. Process for a few seconds to blend, then add the butter. Process for 10 to 20 seconds or until the mixture is like fine crumbs.

Beat the yolks and water together with a fork. With the motor running, pour into the food processor. Process for about 5 seconds or until the dough *just* comes together.

Crumble dough into a 11x7–inch rectangular fluted tart pan with a removable bottom (or use a 12-inch round tart pan). Press dough evenly into pan with your fingers, making sure that the bottom of the crust isn't too thick. Using a fork, prick the dough all over. Press a double-folded piece of foil down into the pan. Bake the pastry for 12 minutes. Reduce oven temperature to 350 degrees. Remove the foil and continue baking for about 10 minutes longer or until pastry is a light golden brown. Cool.

Toss the squash with 1 tablespoon oil; season with salt, pepper, nutmeg, and cumin. Spread out on a parchment-lined rimmed baking sheet. Repeat with the mushrooms on a second baking sheet. Roast for about 25 minutes or until tender. Cool for about 5 minutes.

Sprinkle ¾ cup cheese in the bottom of the pastry crust. Arrange the squash and mushrooms on top, then sprinkle with the remaining ½ cup cheese. Bake the tart for 10 minutes or until the cheese is melted. Sprinkle with herbs and onions. Serve tart warm or at room temperature, cut into slices.

kitchen notes

Arrange the squash as creatively as you like, setting off the mushrooms as a pretty autumn spray—a showy way to use a smaller harvest. If you choose delicata squash, you can scoop out the seeds before slicing if you prefer.

For tiny individual appetizers, press the pastry into a mini muffin tin or individual fluted tartlet molds and prebake like the larger tarts (they'll take less time). Purée the roasted squash, seasoning it with ground nutmeg and cumin. Spoon the purée into the tartlet shells and top with the roasted mushrooms and bits of fresh herb.

mixed mushroom ragoût with sage gremolata

serves 6

2 tablespoons olive oil

1 tablespoon butter

2 pounds mixed fresh wild mushrooms (chanterelles, king boletes, hen of the woods, and/or hedgehogs)

coarse salt and freshly ground pepper to taste

1 small onion, finely chopped

½ cup dry white wine

½ cup Roasted Wild Mushroom Stock (see page 292) or beef broth

2 cups torn baby greens (arugula, kale, or thinly sliced radicchio), if you'd like

½ cup flat-leaf parsley

8 sage leaves

2 cloves garlic

1 tablespoon grated lemon zest

polenta, gnocchi, or pasta

Heat the oil and butter in a large deep skillet over medium-high heat. Add the mushrooms; season with salt and pepper. Cook, stirring frequently, for about 10 minutes. Increase heat to high, add the onion, and continue cooking for about 5 minutes or until the mushrooms are deeply browned.

Stir in the wine; cook until it's evaporated. Add the stock; bring to a boil. Season with salt and pepper. Stir in the greens, if using.

Meanwhile, finely chop the parsley, sage, garlic, and lemon zest together on a cutting board.

Serve the mushrooms, sprinkled with the gremolata, as you prefer over hot cooked or grilled polenta, gnocchi, or pasta.

kitchen notes

This Italian-inspired recipe pretty much writes itself. Savory, fruity, and earthy all at once, it's nearly the best way to enjoy wild mushrooms. Since each mushroom takes its own time to be done, add them to the pan based on how firm they are, especially if you have delicate black trumpets or denser chicken of the woods or lobsters, before melding them together in a slow simmer of wine.

In midwestern Italian neighborhoods, a cache of wild mushrooms simmered up as a ragoût becomes a meal starter for a cacciatore (hunter's stew), a straight-up sauce for sweet potato gnocchi or even a parsnip mash, or an appetizer on top of toasted crusty bread. Or see if you can find some Crescenza-Stracchino, a thick rindless cow's milk cheese with a creamy color and mildly tangy flavor. It's aged only about a week, so its flavor is similar to a Monterey Jack and it's a great melting cheese. Spread some on warm slices of grilled firm polenta with a big spoonful of the earthy mushroom stew.

warm pan-roasted chicken liver & lion's mane salad

serves 2 to 3

olive oil

6 ounces fresh lion's mane mushrooms, torn or sliced into bite-size pieces

2 large shallots, cut into thin wedges

coarse salt and freshly ground pepper to taste

finely chopped fresh rosemary to taste

1 tablespoon butter

½ pound chicken livers, trimmed and halved

2 tablespoons sherry vinegar or white balsamic vinegar

3 cups baby spinach leaves

Heat 1 tablespoon oil in a large skillet over medium-high heat. Sauté the mushrooms for about 6 minutes or until they release their juices. Stir in the shallots and season with salt, pepper, and rosemary. Continue cooking, stirring frequently, for 4 to 5 minutes longer or until the shallots and mushrooms are very tender and browned. Scrape into a shallow serving dish.

Melt butter in skillet over medium-high heat. Add the chicken livers; season with salt and pepper. Cook, turning them, for 3 to 4 minutes or until browned and crisp but still slightly pink in the center. Scrape into the dish with the mushrooms and shallots.

Pour the vinegar, 1 tablespoon oil, and a splash of water into the hot skillet, scraping up the browned bits from the bottom of the pan. To serve, arrange the greens on plates and spoon the liver and mushrooms on top. Drizzle with the pan juices.

kitchen notes

My mother adores chicken livers as much as my dad hates them. I share my mom's taste, so they've been a "mom and me" supper when it's just the two of us. We haven't shared this version of a beloved recipe, spiked with lion's mane mushrooms, but we have a date on the calendar. I like the slight bitterness of lion's mane with liver: there's a full-bodied transformation when they're paired up, balanced with the sweetness of the shallots and pulled together with the pan vinaigrette. The key to great liver is cooking it quickly, until crispy golden and just tender. You can dust the livers with seasoned flour for a light crustiness, but I'm usually satisfied without. I just want that lightly crisp exterior, with a creamy texture and pale pink interior. Deglazing the pan with some sweet sherry or Madeira is a delicious quick finish if you'd like to skip the greens; spoon the livers and mushrooms onto slices of toasted bread instead.

chimichurri-marinated steak with woodland mushrooms

serves 4

½ cup red wine vinegar

I teaspoon coarse salt

4 cloves garlic, finely chopped

I medium shallot, finely chopped

I small red Fresno chile, finely chopped

½ cup finely chopped fresh parsley

½ cup finely chopped fresh cilantro leaves

2 tablespoons finely chopped fresh oregano

½ teaspoon toasted cumin seed

dash red pepper flakes

¾ cup olive oil

2 (1¼–pound) porterhouse steaks (1 inch thick)

¾ pound fresh hen of the woods mushrooms, trimmed and torn into bite-size pieces (or oysters earlier in the summer)

2 tablespoons butter

sprigs fresh thyme to taste

Mix the vinegar, salt, garlic, shallot, and chile in a medium bowl; let stand for 10 minutes while you're chopping up the herbs and toasting the cumin seeds. Stir in the herbs, cumin, and red pepper flakes, then whisk in the oil until well blended. Measure out ½ cup and pour into a small bowl; set aside to serve at the table.

Place the meat and mushrooms in a large glass baking dish; spoon in the rest of the herb mixture, coating the meat and mushrooms. Cover and refrigerate for at least 2 hours, but take them out of the fridge about 30 minutes before cooking so they can warm up a little.

Melt the butter in a heavy wide skillet over medium-high heat. Remove the steaks from the marinade, pat them dry, and cook about 9 minutes, turning once, for medium rare or until done to your taste. Transfer the steaks to a tray and loosely cover with foil.

Remove the mushrooms from the marinade (discard marinade) and sauté for 8 to 10 minutes or until tender and very browned and crisp around the edges.

Serve the steaks sliced and sprinkled with thyme, with the mushrooms and a dish of the reserved chimichurri.

kitchen notes

Cozying up the raw shallots and garlic with vinegar for a few minutes takes away some of their bite, sort of like a quick pickling that allows the strong flavors to infuse into what's basically an herb-heavy vinaigrette. Of course, you can grill the steaks, but the bits of chimichurri that cling to the steaks in combination with the butter in the skillet (a well-seasoned cast-iron or heavy stainless-steel pan is best) is really delicious. Cooking the mushrooms in the same pan is efficient and lets them soak up some of the meat's flavor. I like to stir in some cooked great northern or cranberry beans at the end with a spoonful of the herb sauce.

creamy bucatini with charred garlic & chicken of the woods

serves 4 to 6

8 ounces uncooked bucatini or whole-wheat spaghetti

6 large cloves unpeeled garlic

3 tablespoons olive oil

3 large green onions, chopped (½ cup)

1 pound fresh chicken of the woods mushrooms, trimmed and torn into bite-size pieces

coarse salt and freshly ground pepper to taste

1½ cups chicken broth

1½ cups heavy cream

fresh basil leaves to taste

Cook the pasta in a large pot of salted boiling water until al dente; drain well.

Meanwhile, heat up a large deep skillet over high heat. Toss the unpeeled garlic cloves in the dry pan and allow them to cook, shaking the pan frequently, for 2 to 3 minutes or until blackened on their flat sides. Cool them, then squeeze out the cloves and finely chop. Set aside.

Heat the oil in the skillet over medium-high heat. Add the onions; sauté for 1 minute. Stir in the mushrooms; season with salt and pepper. Sauté for about 10 minutes, stirring frequently, until nearly tender and lightly charred around the edges.

Pour in the broth; reduce the heat and simmer for 5 minutes. Add the cream and reserved garlic; simmer for about 3 minutes. Gently stir in the cooked pasta and toss until it's well coated. Serve with a shower of torn basil and freshly ground pepper.

kitchen notes

A simple plate of creamy pasta takes advantage of the meatiness of chicken of the woods, offering it a starring role. I really like this method of taming garlic's bite, too, giving the cloves a roasted edge without turning on the oven—sort of like the classic technique for *oignon brûlé*, or charring aromatics to deepen and sweeten their flavor—infusing the light creamy sauce without overwhelming it, rounding out the overall savory richness of the dish.

creamy shaggy mane pot pies

serves 4

1 sheet frozen puff pastry from a 1-pound box, thawed in the refrigerator overnight

8 tablespoons butter, divided

1 medium fennel bulb, trimmed, cored, and chopped

¾ cup red pearl onions, peeled and cut into quarters

1 cup sliced carrots

1 cup sliced celery

1 pound fresh shaggy mane and/or giant puffball mushrooms, chopped

coarse salt and freshly ground pepper to taste

⅓ cup unbleached all-purpose flour

3 cups chicken stock

½ cup half-and-half

2 tablespoons fresh marjoram leaves, coarsely chopped, or 2 teaspoons dried, crushed

1 tablespoon fresh thyme leaves or 1 teaspoon dried, crushed

½ teaspoon celery seed

1 egg, lightly beaten with 1 teaspoon water

Roll out the pastry a bit, then cut into quarters. Lay the pieces on a tray and cover with plastic; refrigerate until ready to use.

Heat oven to 400 degrees. Melt 2 tablespoons butter in a large skillet over medium-high heat. Sauté the fennel, onions, carrots, and celery for 10 to 15 minutes, stirring frequently, until tender. Scrape into a bowl.

Melt 2 tablespoons butter in skillet over medium-high heat. Add the mushrooms and sauté for 6 to 8 minutes or until tender and beginning to brown. Scrape into the bowl with the vegetables; season mixture with salt and pepper.

Melt the remaining 4 tablespoons butter in the skillet over medium-high heat. Stir in the flour; whisk until well blended. Reduce heat to medium-low and cook until mixture turns golden brown. Whisk in 1 cup stock until smooth; stir in the rest of the stock, along with the half-and-half, herbs, and celery seed. Bring to a boil, stirring constantly, for 2 to 3 minutes or until thickened. Season with salt and pepper.

Return the mushrooms and vegetables to the sauce in the skillet; stir until well blended. Spoon the mixture into 4 (12-ounce) ramekins or individual baking dishes. Top each ramekin with a square of pastry, pressing down around edges to seal. Cut slits in the pastry and brush with the beaten egg wash. Bake for 20 to 25 minutes or until the pastry is puffed and golden brown.

kitchen notes

Frozen puff pastry is an elegant shortcut for homemade pot pies, but feel free to substitute your favorite pie pastry or even a cut-out biscuit or drop dumpling to finish these off. A big spoonful of mashed potatoes on top, creating small mushroom shepherd's pies, would be comforting in the autumn. If you choose a drop dumpling or mashed potatoes, reduce the bake time by a good amount—just go until the topping is golden.

forest feast hot dish with frizzled onions

serves 8

1 cup uncooked pearl barley

1 cup uncooked wild rice, hand-harvested if you can get some

coarse salt

2 tablespoons olive oil

1 medium onion, thinly sliced

8 slices thick-sliced hickory-smoked bacon, chopped

2 large leeks, halved lengthwise, rinsed well, and sliced crosswise

1¼ pounds mixed fresh wild mushrooms (chicken of the woods, hen of the woods, king bolete, and/or chanterelle), trimmed and sliced or torn

1 tablespoon chopped fresh sage leaves, plus sprigs for garnish

2 teaspoons lightly chopped fresh thyme leaves, plus sprigs for garnish

1½ cups (6 ounces) shredded fontina cheese

freshly ground pepper to taste

Mix the barley and wild rice in a large saucepan; cover with water and add a good teaspoon of salt. Bring to a boil; reduce heat and partially cover. Cook for about 45 minutes or until tender; drain any excess water. Spoon into a large bowl.

Meanwhile, heat the oil in a large heavy skillet over medium-high heat. Add the onion; sauté, stirring frequently, until golden and crisp. Remove to a paper towel–lined plate; set aside.

Heat oven to 375 degrees. Lightly grease a 3-quart ceramic baking dish; set aside. Cook the bacon over medium-high heat until crisp; remove the bacon with a slotted spoon, leaving the fat in the skillet. Add the bacon pieces to the cooked grains.

Add the leeks and mushrooms to the bacon fat; sauté for 10 to 12 minutes, stirring frequently, until tender. Scrape into the bowl with the grain mixture. Stir in the chopped herbs and cheese. Season with a little more salt and lots of ground pepper.

Spoon into the prepared baking dish; cover with foil. Place in the oven and bake for 15 to 20 minutes or until hot and the cheese is melted. Serve topped with the frizzled onions and sprigs of sage and thyme.

kitchen notes

I've been a whole-grain disciple for most of my grown-up years, eschewing many "white" ingredients. Barley, a highly underrated grain, is important in immigrant cuisines and is often paired with mushrooms. I've always thought of wild rice as the closest thing to a standard-bearer for an iconic upper midwestern food. I've carried it abroad as a regional gift to loads of friends—and found an enthusiastic audience for it in other rice-loving places like northern Italy and Japan. When I was studying at a French cooking school years ago, wild rice was considered very exotic, with the moniker *riz sauvage*. Actually a wild grass, it's traditionally hand harvested by Native Americans, and though it's now farmed in California, the real stuff is more interesting, with an earthier aroma and texture—well worth its high price.

I think this combination is nice enough for a holiday buffet or fancy make-and-take gathering. Extend the season to late fall by substituting rehydrated dried king boletes and lobster mushrooms.

game hens with creamy maitake pasta

serves 4 to 6

2–3 (24-ounce) Rock Cornish game hens, thawed if frozen

olive oil

1 tablespoon dried rosemary, crushed

coarse salt and freshly ground pepper to taste

12 ounces uncooked pappardelle or long fusilli pasta

2 tablespoons butter

2 medium leeks, halved lengthwise, rinsed well, and sliced crosswise

3 cloves garlic, finely chopped

1 pound fresh hen of the woods (maitake) mushrooms, torn into pieces

½ cup heavy cream

¼ teaspoon freshly ground nutmeg

fresh rosemary and sage leaves as desired

Heat oven to 425 degrees. Rub game hens with 2 tablespoons oil and season with rosemary, salt, and pepper. Arrange on a large parchment-lined rimmed baking sheet. Roast hens about 50 minutes or until juices run clear when the thickest part of the thighs is pierced with a knife.

Meanwhile, cook pasta according to package directions; drain and keep warm. Heat butter and 1 tablespoon oil in a large deep skillet over medium-high heat. Add leeks; sauté for 3 minutes. Add garlic and mushrooms; sauté for 5 minutes or until tender. Season with salt and pepper. Stir in cream, nutmeg, and warm pasta; toss to coat with sauce.

Cut hens in half; serve on a bed of the creamy pasta and mushrooms. Sprinkle with fresh herbs.

kitchen notes

The darker meat of any small roasted game bird is complemented by a stylish pasta that's lightly coated with an herbal cream and enriched with quickly sautéed mushrooms and leeks. Domestic Rock Cornish hens are easy to come by, but wild grouse, pheasant, quail, or partridge would be even better, with flavors to match the wildness of the mushrooms. I really like this dish for company, with a big bowl of slightly bitter, cool-weather greens (baby kale, beet greens, frisée, radicchio, or arugula) tossed with a sweet citrus vinaigrette. The astringency of the greens balances the richness of the darker meat, mushrooms, and cream.

chicken (of the woods) tikka masala

serves 6

1 pound fresh chicken of the woods mushrooms, torn or chopped into bite-size pieces

1 tablespoon peanut or canola oil

1 tablespoon ground coriander

1½ teaspoons ground cumin

1½ teaspoons paprika

1 teaspoon garam masala

½ teaspoon ground cardamom

¼ teaspoon ground nutmeg

¼ teaspoon cayenne

1 tablespoon grated peeled fresh gingerroot (about a 1-inch piece)

2 cloves garlic, finely chopped

¼ cup ghee or clarified butter

1 large white onion, finely chopped

2 cups canned tomato purée

¾ cup heavy cream

½ cup Roasted Wild Mushroom Stock (see page 292)

½ cup plain Greek yogurt

1 cup chopped fresh cilantro leaves, divided

1¼ teaspoons kosher salt

½ teaspoon freshly ground black pepper

hot cooked brown basmati rice or warm naan flatbread

Heat a large skillet over medium-high heat. Sauté the mushrooms in the dry pan until they begin to stick, then add the oil. Continue cooking until mushrooms begin to crisp around the edges. Set aside.

Mix the coriander, cumin, paprika, garam masala, cardamom, nutmeg, cayenne, ginger, and garlic in a small dish. Warm the ghee in a large saucepan over medium heat; sauté the onion for 15 to 20 minutes or until it begins to caramelize.

Stir in the spice mixture, reduce heat, and stir in the tomato purée, cream, and mushroom stock. Bring to a boil; cook and stir for 10 minutes or until slightly thickened. Reduce heat and stir in the yogurt and sautéed mushrooms. Cook and stir for 5 minutes longer. Remove from heat and stir in half of the cilantro and the salt and pepper. Serve over rice, sprinkled with the rest of the cilantro.

kitchen notes

Michael and I talked about how we like to make curry-style dishes, sometimes straight from a jar (Indian simmer sauces can be quite good) when we need a shortcut, sometimes toasting and grinding whole spices when we can be leisurely. This recipe hits the middle mark—using the ground spices buys you a little time and the freedom to tailor the blend to your own taste. Swap in hen of the woods for the COW if you'd like: both mushrooms add a great meatiness to the dish. In India, chunks of real chicken are marinated and grilled over a smoky fire, then served in a casserole with a small foil packet of smoldering charcoal; likewise, you could try stirring in lightly smoked mushroom chunks.

coconut-braised chicken of the woods

serves 4 to 6

2 tablespoons olive oil

1½ pounds fresh chicken of the woods mushrooms, trimmed and chopped into 1-inch pieces

coarse salt and freshly ground pepper

½ pound fresh bulk chorizo sausage

1 onion, thinly sliced

1 tablespoon grated fresh gingerroot

2 cloves garlic, finely chopped

1 chipotle chile in adobo, chopped, plus 1 teaspoon sauce

3 cups unsweetened coconut milk

1 pound small Yukon gold potatoes, cut into quarters

2 large limes

1 teaspoon cumin seed, toasted and crushed

hot cooked brown rice

chopped fresh cilantro and oregano leaves

Heat oven to 400 degrees. Heat the oil in a large Dutch oven or enameled casserole with an ovenproof lid over medium-high heat. Sauté the mushrooms for about 10 minutes; season with salt and pepper. Scrape into a bowl.

Add the sausage and onion to the pan and cook, stirring to break up the meat, until the onion is translucent. Stir in the ginger, garlic, chile, and adobo sauce; cook until fragrant. Stir in the coconut milk, potatoes, and mushrooms. Bring to a simmer. Cover and bake for about 45 minutes.

Cut 1 lime into wedges and put into a small dish for the table. Grate the zest from the second lime into a second small dish and mix with the cumin and 1 teaspoon coarse salt. Squeeze the juice from the second lime into the casserole, stirring until blended. Serve the stew over rice, sprinkled with the cumin-lime salt and lots of fresh herbs.

kitchen notes

Look for a nice fruiting of chicken that's a good size but still moist, though if you discover a larger one this is a good tenderizing dish. Come in from a chilly hunt and heat up the oven for a nice braise to warm up a brisk autumn afternoon.

For the chipotle in adobo—which are just smoked dried ripe jalapeño chiles in a spiced sauce—buy a small can. Chop what's left in the can and spoon it into an ice cube tray or into small mounds on a baking sheet. Freeze them, and then you'll have a bit of smoky heat to pop into a soup (like the Spiced Roasted Corn Soup with Mushroom Duxelles, see page 158) or another oven braise.

hearty mushroom & vegetable zuppa

serves 6

1 tablespoon olive oil

6 ounces uncured smoked bacon, chopped

½ pound fresh king bolete and/or hen of the woods mushrooms, trimmed and chopped

1 small onion, chopped

2 medium carrots, chopped

1 fresh fennel bulb, trimmed and chopped

1 small zucchini, chopped

6 cloves garlic, finely chopped

3 tablespoons chopped fresh rosemary leaves

coarse salt and freshly ground pepper to taste

½ cup dry red wine

6 cups beef stock

1 (14.5-ounce) can fire-roasted diced tomatoes, undrained

2 cups chopped or torn dry crusty bread

1 (15-ounce) can garbanzo beans, rinsed and drained

1 (15-ounce) can great northern beans, rinsed and drained

4 cups chopped kale or Swiss chard

freshly grated Parmesan cheese, red pepper flakes

Heat oil in a large Dutch oven or soup kettle over medium-high heat. Add bacon; cook and stir about 5 minutes or until crisp and fat is rendered. Remove bacon to a plate; set aside.

Add mushrooms to pan; sauté until their juices are released. Add onion, carrots, fennel, zucchini, garlic, and rosemary; season with salt and pepper. Sauté vegetables for 8 to 10 minutes longer, stirring frequently.

Pour wine into pan; cook and stir to scrape up browned bits. Add the stock and tomatoes with their juices. Bring soup to a boil; reduce heat and simmer for a few minutes. Stir in the bread and beans.

Add the kale to the pan; cook, partially covered, until wilted. Serve soup hot, in shallow bowls, sprinkled with the crisp bacon and topped with cheese, red pepper flakes, and a good drizzle of olive oil.

kitchen notes

Call it what you will—a variation on minestrone, ribollita, or just a "whatever is left in the veggie crisper" stew—but this recipe offers a reliable design for making the best use of loose mushrooms, garden stragglers, or a last CSA box. Mix up what you throw in: a handful of chopped string beans, a stalk or two of celery, or a few nearly overripe tomatoes. The mushrooms add a meaty note with the bacon, boosting the appeal of stewed vegetables.

hens and greens with butter-steamed eggs

serves 4

olive oil

½ cup broken walnut pieces

¼ teaspoon toasted ground cumin

dash cayenne

1 large leek, halved lengthwise, rinsed well, and sliced crosswise

3 cloves garlic, finely chopped

½ pound fresh hen of the woods mushrooms, torn into bite-size pieces

coarse salt or freshly ground smoked salt and pepper to taste

10 ounces baby greens (kale and/or spinach)

butter

4 large eggs

torn fresh cilantro sprigs and red wine vinegar to taste

Heat 2 teaspoons oil in a large deep skillet over medium heat. Add walnuts, cumin, and cayenne; cook and stir for about 2 minutes or until fragrant. Pour into a shallow dish; cool.

Heat 4 teaspoons oil in the skillet over medium-high heat. Add the leeks and garlic; sauté for 3 minutes or until softened. Add the mushrooms; season with salt and pepper. Sauté, stirring occasionally, for about 8 minutes. Stir in the greens; cook until wilted. Spoon mushroom-greens mixture onto 4 plates.

Meanwhile, melt a small knob of butter in a small (7-inch) skillet over medium heat. Break an egg into the skillet; season with salt and pepper. Spoon a few tablespoons of water over the egg; cover the skillet and steam until the egg white is firm but the yolk is still soft. Slide the egg on top of a plate of greens. Repeat with the rest of the eggs.

Top each plate with some torn cilantro, a splash of vinegar, and a sprinkle of spiced nuts.

kitchen notes

I grew up on steamed eggs, complete with a runny yolk, which becomes the heart of an instant sauce for the meaty hens and barely tender greens. If you'd like to make this a one-disher, go ahead and break the eggs on top of the mushrooms and greens while they're still in the large skillet. Pour in some broth and add a few tablespoons of butter, cover the pan, and let the steam cook the eggs to the doneness you like. Serve straight from the pan, finished with the cilantro, vinegar, and walnuts.

indulgent stovetop mac & cheese

serves 6

6 tablespoons butter

1 cup fresh bread crumbs or panko

¼ cup (1 ounce) grated Parmesan cheese

2 cloves garlic, finely chopped

½ pound fresh lobster, king bolete, and/or hen of the woods mushrooms, trimmed and sliced or chopped

coarse salt and freshly ground pepper to taste

½ cup unbleached all-purpose flour

6 cups milk (or 4 cups half-and-half plus 2 cups milk)

12 ounces uncooked fusilli pasta

3 cups (12 ounces) shredded fontina cheese

1 cup (4 ounces) shredded smoked provolone

thinly sliced fresh basil leaves

Melt butter in a large deep ovenproof skillet over medium-high heat. Mix the bread crumbs and Parmesan in a small bowl. Stir in 1 tablespoon melted butter. Set aside.

Add the garlic and the mushrooms to the rest of the butter in the skillet. Sauté for about 8 minutes or until tender and browned. Season with salt and pepper. Stir in the flour; cook and stir for 1 minute. Stir in the milk; bring to a simmer.

Stir in the pasta and cook over medium-low heat for about 8 minutes, stirring frequently, until al dente. Stir in the cheeses until melted.

Heat the broiler to high. Sprinkle the bread crumbs evenly over the pasta. Place under the broiler for 1 to 2 minutes or until golden brown. Sprinkle each serving with some basil.

kitchen notes

I'm generally not a huge fan of truffle-flavored products, but a quick dribble or two of truffle oil would really be good if you have any around—or maybe a little Toasted Mushroom–Chile Dipping Oil (see page 297). There aren't many folks I know who would turn up their noses at a mac 'n' cheese stuffed with exotic mushrooms and rich enough for a date night.

midwestern sweet & sour ratatouille

serves 6

2 medium sweet bell peppers (red, green, or yellow)

1 pound plum tomatoes

8 cloves unpeeled garlic

¼ cup olive oil

1 pound mixed fresh wild mushrooms (giant puffball, king bolete, hen of the woods), trimmed and coarsely chopped

2 red onions, coarsely chopped

2 small eggplant, coarsely chopped

2 medium zucchini, coarsely chopped

coarse salt and freshly ground pepper to taste

2 tablespoons sugar or to taste

2 tablespoons red wine vinegar or to taste

⅓ cup chopped green olives

2 tablespoons small capers

2 tablespoons chopped mixed fresh herbs (rosemary, basil, summer savory, peppermint, thyme, lavender)

Heat broiler to high. Arrange the bell peppers, tomatoes, and garlic cloves on a parchment-lined rimmed baking sheet. Place under the broiler and cook, turning frequently, until charred and skins have burst. Remove from the oven; cover with foil for 5 minutes to allow the vegetables to steam.

Meanwhile, heat oil in a Dutch oven or large deep pan over medium-high heat. Sauté the mushrooms and onions for 10 minutes, stirring frequently, until tender.

Uncover the broiled vegetables and peel the waxy skin from the bell peppers and the skins from the tomatoes; squeeze the garlic from their papery covering. Coarsely chop everything and scrape, with all the juices, into the pan with the mushrooms and onions.

Add the eggplant and zucchini to the pan and season well with salt and pepper; lower the heat to medium and simmer the stew, stirring occasionally, for 20 to 25 minutes or until everything is very tender.

Stir in the sugar and vinegar (add more sugar and/or vinegar to meet your taste); simmer for 10 minutes longer. Add the olives, capers, and herbs. Serve hot or at room temperature.

kitchen notes

As reliable as the sunrise, the early fall bursts with the ripening of tomatoes, sweet bell peppers, eggplants, and more and more zucchini. And the tradition for stewing up the late-harvest plenty is widespread, especially in the southern Mediterranean but just as much here in the center of the United States. I know gardeners who grow only the ingredients for a French ratatouille, and I particularly like the Spanish twist of adding capers, olives, and a bit of sugar to smooth the acid of the tomatoes. Since now is the time for a real explosion of wild mushrooms, stewing them up in this mélange deepens and rounds out the flavor—which only gets better if this dish is made ahead and reheated. Add some sliced grilled sausages, or for a veggie-forward supper just spoon it over hot cooked pasta with lots of grated Parmesan or crumbly aged goat cheese.

marcela's marinated mushrooms

serves 8

2 medium yellow or red onions, halved and sliced

4 cloves garlic, sliced

2½ cups canola, corn, or sunflower oil

¼ cup extra-virgin olive oil

1 pound fresh king bolete, hen of the woods, chanterelle, or hedgehog mushrooms, halved or thickly sliced if large

¼ pound fresh hen of the woods mushrooms, torn into 1½– to 2-inch pieces

1½ cups dried wild blueberries, dark raisins, or currants

¾ cup cider vinegar

½ cup dry white wine

2 teaspoons smoked paprika

coarse salt and freshly ground pepper to taste

fresh oregano leaves to taste

sliced fresh jalapeño or Fresno chiles, if you'd like some spice

Cover the onions and garlic with oils in a deep wide pan or stockpot. Bring to a simmer over medium heat. Cook, stirring occasionally, for 5 to 8 minutes or until nearly tender.

Stir in mushrooms; gently simmer for 10 minutes. Add the blueberries; cook 5 minutes longer or until the mushrooms are tender.

Stir in the vinegar and wine; season with the paprika, salt, and pepper. Cool; cover and refrigerate for at least 4 hours or overnight. Use a slotted spoon to transfer the mushrooms to a serving bowl or spoon into jars. Sprinkle with oregano and hot chiles. Refrigerate for up to 2 weeks.

kitchen notes

My dear friend Marcela Sorondo, a cookbook writer and food stylist in Buenos Aires, made these mushrooms one evening for us on a visit to the States. As she generously poured oil over the onions, garlic, and mushrooms—that night it was a combination of oysters and chanterelles—and gently poached them, I knew the result would be a great variation on a favorite 1950s cocktail party standard. It's also a longtime Eastern European method for preserving a very seasonal harvest. The subtle sweetness the blueberries infuse into the marinade balances the vinegar. Dennis's family likes to spoon the mushrooms onto grilled bruschetta with garlic-infused summer tomatoes dressed with a splash of white balsamic vinegar.

pan-seared pheasant with mushroom & creamy port sauce

serves 4

2 whole pheasants (about 3¼ pounds total)

olive oil

coarse salt and freshly ground pepper to taste

½ pound fresh hen of the woods and/or oyster mushrooms, torn into pieces

3 large shallots, cut into wedges

½ cup ruby port

3 tablespoons red currant jelly

¼ cup heavy cream

Pull the skin from the pheasants; cut them into pieces, leaving the breasts whole or cutting them in half. Heat a large deep skillet over medium-high heat; add 2 tablespoons oil. Season the pheasant pieces with salt and pepper; cook in skillet, turning frequently, until well browned. Transfer them to a plate.

Add 2 tablespoons oil to pan; stir in the mushrooms. Sauté about 8 minutes, stirring occasionally, until browned. Stir in shallots; cook about 3 minutes. Reduce heat to medium-low; stir in the port, scraping to loosen the browned bits in the pan; simmer for 1 minute. Stir in the jelly until melted, then add the cream.

Return the pheasant pieces to pan with any juices. Bring to a simmer; partially cover the pan and cook for 10 to 15 minutes or until pheasant is no longer pink near the bone. Adjust seasonings; serve pheasant with mushrooms and sauce.

kitchen notes
Each fall I happily anticipate sharing in the domestic bounty of talented gardeners and imaginative makers I know: their luscious preserves, tangy pickles, and relishes, both sweet and savory. My creative friend Susan Telleen makes sparkling jars of blushing jelly from the currants in her yard; her patient care and artistry in making jellies is only matched by her lovely drawings and watercolors. This classic pairing of wild pheasant and a currant-tinged port sauce is extraordinary when some wild mushrooms join in. If you have bird hunters in your world you can substitute grouse or even duck breasts for the pheasant—and some thinly sliced king bolete mushrooms would be fantastic in place of or added to the hens and oysters.

pork tenderloin with black trumpet sorghum & ground cherry salsa

serves 6

for the pilaf & pork

olive oil

1 cup sorghum grain

3 cups mushroom (see page 292) or beef stock

coarse salt and freshly ground pepper to taste

3 green onions, chopped

½ pound fresh black trumpet mushrooms, rinsed and torn into strips

½ cup sorghum syrup or mild molasses

½ cup apple cider vinegar

2 medium pork tenderloins (about 1¾ pounds total)

for the salsa

1½ cups ground cherries, husked, rinsed, and halved or quartered

½ cup finely chopped red bell pepper

⅓ cup finely chopped red onion

⅓ cup finely chopped fresh mint

1 jalapeño chile, finely chopped

1 tablespoon sorghum syrup or honey

1 tablespoon apple cider vinegar

Heat 1 tablespoon oil in a large saucepan over medium-high heat. Add the sorghum; lightly toast it (it might pop a little) for a minute or so. Stir in the stock; season with salt and pepper. Bring to a boil; reduce heat to low. Cover and simmer for 55 minutes to an hour or until tender.

Heat 1 tablespoon oil in a heavy ovenproof skillet over medium-high heat. Sauté the onions for 30 seconds, then stir in the mushrooms. Cook for just a few minutes, until wilted and tender. Season lightly with salt and pepper. Scrape into the saucepan with the cooked sorghum. Cover and keep warm.

Meanwhile, heat oven to 425 degrees. To make the glaze for the pork, mix the ½ cup sorghum syrup and ½ cup vinegar in a small saucepan over medium-high heat. Bring to a boil, then reduce heat to medium and cook, stirring occasionally, for 4 to 6 minutes or until slightly thickened.

Heat 1 tablespoon oil in the heavy skillet over medium-high heat. Season the pork with salt and pepper. Brown the meat well on all sides; brush the pork with some of the glaze.

Place the skillet in the oven; roast the pork for 10 minutes. Brush the pork with more glaze and roast for 10 to 15 minutes longer or until just barely pink in the center. Remove from oven and tent with foil; let stand for 10 minutes before slicing. Heat any remaining glaze until it's boiling.

To make the salsa, mix all the ingredients together in a small serving bowl. Serve the pork sliced, with the last of the glaze spooned over, on a bed of the sorghum-mushroom pilaf, with the salsa alongside.

kitchen notes

Ground cherries are like small cherry tomatoes with a sweet, complex, fruity flavor—great with both sweet and savory. I like pairing the salsa with the richness of the pork and black trumpets, which have their own delicate fruitiness. The sorghum syrup, which has a dark sweetness, just works with the mushrooms and ground cherries.

I grew up using sweet sorghum syrup in a secret (at the behest of my grandmother) family cookie recipe. My

(Continued next page)

great-grandmother, a talented home baker in Nebraska, bought her syrup from a mill in Waconia, Iowa. These days sorghum, primarily as a syrup like molasses, is more known for its southern traditions. Historically grown as fodder for livestock in other parts of the world, forage sorghum is still cultivated in Texas, Kansas, and Nebraska. During the fall baking season, I often run across syrups that are a blend of sorghum with high-fructose corn syrup, but some years I can source it in whole-foods stores and always online. If I order it I err on the high side, so I have some in my pantry.

Whole-grain sorghum (which looks sort of like pearl couscous) is part of the discovery of lesser-known gluten-free grains—just one more choice for a unique pilaf. Like other whole grains it takes nearly an hour to cook, but it's a great candidate as a do-ahead side dish in a slow cooker or sped up in a pressure cooker. Amaranth grain, which looks like a tiny version of quinoa, would also be an interesting choice for a fluffy pilaf and takes half the time to cook.

wild mushroom–eggplant lasagna

serves 6

2 large eggplants, trimmed and cut lengthwise into ¾-inch-thick slices

coarse salt

½ cup (½ ounce) dried mushrooms

1 cup chicken broth

olive oil

4 cloves garlic, finely chopped

1½ pounds mixed fresh wild mushrooms (chanterelles, hedgehog, hen of the woods, or king boletes), sliced

¼ cup butter

3 tablespoons unbleached all-purpose flour

1½ cups milk

1 teaspoon finely chopped fresh thyme leaves

freshly ground pepper to taste

freshly grated nutmeg to taste

12 fresh basil leaves, torn, plus more for garnish

12 ounces fresh mozzarella cheese, sliced

¾ cup (3 ounces) grated Parmesan cheese

Lightly sprinkle the eggplant on both sides with salt. Leave in a colander for about 40 minutes to drain. Meanwhile, rehydrate the dried mushrooms in the chicken broth.

Heat 2 tablespoons oil in a large heavy skillet over medium heat. Sauté the garlic for 1 minute; stir in the fresh mushrooms. Cook, stirring frequently, for about 8 minutes or until they release their juices and are brown. Scrape into a bowl.

Pat the eggplant dry with a paper towel. Lightly brush one side of each slice with oil; sauté oiled-side down, one layer at a time, for 4 to 6 minutes or until golden. Transfer to a plate; repeat with the rest of the slices. Scoop the rehydrated mushrooms from the chicken broth; chop and add to sautéed mushrooms. Strain chicken broth through a fine cheesecloth-lined sieve or a coffee filter; set aside.

Heat oven to 375 degrees. Lightly grease a 3-quart baking dish. Melt butter in a medium saucepan over medium heat. Whisk in the flour; cook and stir for 2 to 3 minutes. Gradually whisk in the milk and the strained chicken broth, stirring for about 10 minutes or until smooth and thickened. Season with thyme, salt, pepper, and nutmeg.

Layer half of the eggplant, slightly overlapping the slices, in the baking dish. Spoon half of the mushrooms evenly on top. Spoon half of the white sauce over and scatter half of the basil on top. Cover with half of the mozzarella slices and half of the Parmesan. Repeat the layers. Bake for 25 to 30 minutes or until golden and bubbling. Serve sprinkled with more fresh basil.

kitchen notes

This is really a *gratin* dish—vegetables layered with a mushroom-infused white sauce and cheese. But I'm loosely calling it a lasagna since I bypass the pasta and layer in thick planks of browned eggplant in its stead.

roasted brussels sprouts & winter squash with smoky maple lobster bacon

serves 4

½ pound Brussels sprouts, halved

olive oil

coarse salt and freshly ground pepper to taste

1 medium thin-skinned winter squash (acorn or delicata), halved and sliced crosswise; no need to peel or seed

2 tablespoons butter

1 large tangerine or medium orange, zested and juiced

¼ teaspoon freshly grated nutmeg

Smoky Maple Lobster Bacon (see page 294)

Heat oven to 425 degrees. Line 2 large rimmed baking sheets with parchment. Toss the sprouts with 1 tablespoon oil and season with salt and pepper. Spread out on one of the baking sheets. Place the squash slices on the second baking sheet; brush with 1 tablespoon oil and season with salt and pepper. Roast the vegetables for 25 to 30 minutes or until tender and browned. Arrange the vegetables on a large serving plate.

Melt the butter in a small saucepan; stir in the tangerine zest, juice, and nutmeg. Spoon over the vegetables. Sprinkle mushroom bacon on top.

kitchen notes

I have long loved very basic, English-style boiled Brussels sprouts—weird, right?—and have felt alone in this love most of my life. And then cooks started roasting the spouts; now they have a whole new obsessive fan base. A good roasting allows their bitterness to fall away and their outer leaves to get crispy and caramelize a bit around the edges. Snuggled up to tender-sweet winter squash and smoky mushroom bacon, these are not your grandmother's boiled sprouts anymore.

If you have a predilection for another type of squash—buttercup, kabocha, kuri—go ahead and use them, peeled and cut into chunks similar in size to the Brussels sprouts.

sausages with caramelized mushrooms, tomatoes & mustardy vinaigrette

serves 4

2 tablespoons finely chopped shallots

2 tablespoons red wine vinegar

2 tablespoons whole-grain mustard

2 tablespoons Dijon mustard

⅓ cup plus 2 tablespoons olive oil

coarse salt and freshly ground pepper to taste

1 small onion, sliced

½ pound mixed fresh wild mushrooms (oyster, chanterelle, hen of the woods), sliced

4 fully cooked cured bratwurst or bison sausages (¾ pound total)

1 cup mixed color cherry tomatoes, halved

fresh sage leaves to taste

soft-cooked polenta

Mix the shallots and vinegar in a medium bowl; let stand 5 minutes. Stir in both mustards, then whisk in ⅓ cup oil until emulsified. Season with salt and pepper. Set aside.

Heat 2 tablespoons oil in a cast-iron or heavy deep skillet over medium-high heat. Add onions; season with salt and pepper. Sauté for 2 minutes. Stir in mushrooms; reduce heat to medium and cook for 10 to 12 minutes, until they release their juices and become browned and crisp around the edges.

Add the sausages, tomatoes, and sage to the pan. Cook, stirring frequently, until sausages are heated through. Serve sausages, mushrooms, and vegetables over polenta with a spoonful of the mustard vinaigrette.

kitchen notes

A cast-iron skillet is one of the most useful pieces of cooking equipment. Inexpensive and versatile, when thoroughly seasoned it can go from stovetop to oven to grill as you need it—and it conducts heat well so your food cooks evenly.

Add a slice of Compound Wild Mushroom Herb Butter (see page 289) to the warm polenta if you've got some stashed in your fridge.

balsamic shallot–stuffed porcini caps

serves 8

16 large fresh king bolete (porcini) mushrooms

olive oil

3 tablespoons butter

6 large shallots, cut into thin wedges

3 tablespoons honey

3 tablespoons aged balsamic vinegar

coarse salt and freshly ground pepper to taste

4 ounces crumbled blue cheese

⅓ cup finely chopped toasted walnuts

flowering garden thyme, if you have any

Heat grill to medium. Trim the stems from the mushrooms and finely chop; set aside. Brush the caps lightly with oil. Place on the grill, stem-side up. Cover and cook about 10 to 15 minutes or until tender and browned.

Meanwhile, melt the butter in a large skillet over medium-high heat. Add the mushroom stems, shallots, and honey. Cook, stirring often, for about 15 minutes or until the shallots begin to brown. Stir in the balsamic vinegar, salt, and pepper.

Spoon the mushroom-shallot mixture on top of the grilled caps. Sprinkle with cheese, walnuts, and thyme leaves and blossoms.

kitchen notes

Michael discovered and delivered an impressive and gorgeous cache of king boletes, just the right size to grill and top with caramelized shallots and blue cheese. Salty-crisp prosciutto shards add just a little more sparkle: Bake thinly sliced prosciutto on a parchment-lined baking sheet at 350 degrees for about 8 minutes. Let them cool, then break into pieces to garnish each mushroom cap. If heating up the grill isn't in the cards, just bake the mushroom caps at 375 degrees for 15 to 20 minutes or until they are tender.

puffball parmigiana

serves 8

1½ pounds fresh giant puffball mushrooms (best to have a couple of smaller ones versus 1 large one)

2 (28-ounce) cans whole San Marzano tomatoes, undrained

3 cloves garlic, crushed in a garlic press or very finely chopped

2 sprigs fresh rosemary, leaves stripped and chopped

1 cup Porcini-Rosemary Crumb Coating (see page 288) or plain dried bread crumbs

1 cup (4 ounces) grated Parmigiano-Reggiano or Pecorino Romano cheese, divided

1 teaspoon fennel seed, crushed

½ teaspoon dried Italian seasoning, crushed

coarse salt and freshly ground pepper to taste

3 large eggs, lightly beaten

1 cup canola or grapeseed oil

1 pound part-skim mozzarella cheese, thinly sliced

Heat oven to 400 degrees. Slice the mushrooms into ½-inch rounds. Nick the edges of each slice and peel off the outer leathery skin. Cut the rounds in half if they're more than 6 inches across.

Place tomatoes, garlic, and rosemary in a large saucepan; bring to a boil. Reduce heat and simmer for 30 minutes or until thickened. Break up larger tomato chunks with the back of a spoon.

Place the crumb coating or bread crumbs, ½ cup Parmesan cheese, herbs, salt, and pepper in a shallow dish. Put eggs in another shallow dish. Dip the mushroom slices in the egg, then dredge in the crumb coating. Lay on a tray.

Heat the oil in a large deep pan over medium-high heat. Carefully fry the mushroom slices, in batches, for about 6 minutes or until golden brown and tender. Drain on a paper towel–lined tray.

Spread 1 cup of the tomato sauce in a 3-quart baking dish. Arrange half of the mushroom slices, overlapping, on top. Spoon in 2 cups of the tomato sauce and layer with half of the mozzarella. Repeat with the rest of the mushroom slices, sauce, and mozzarella. Sprinkle with the last ½ cup Parmesan.

Bake for about 30 minutes or until bubbling and cheese is golden. Let cool for a few minutes before serving.

kitchen notes

It's an easy swap to crumb coat and fry sliced puffballs in lieu of eggplant: both have a slightly spongy texture, carry a mild flavor that shines when browned and crisped, and happily meld into a spicy tomato-herb confit. Use an oil with a high smoke point—like the suggested canola or grapeseed—to fry the coated mushrooms. Add some clarified butter to the oil to boost the natural nuttiness of the mushrooms and deepen the flavor underpinnings of this irresistibly gooey casserole. To really maintain the crunchy exterior of the mushrooms, skip the casserole layering and just plate the hot mushroom slices on big spoonfuls of sauce, sprinkled with cheese.

spiced & crunchy mushroom bites with creamy cilantro dip

serves 8 as a snack or appetizer

for the mushrooms

3 tablespoons slivered almonds

3 tablespoons sesame seed

1½ cups cornflakes or cornflake crumbs

coarse salt and crushed red pepper to taste

½ cup unbleached all-purpose flour

2 large eggs

1 pound fresh chicken of the woods or giant puffball mushrooms, cut into ¾-inch chunks

¼ cup olive oil

for the dip

1 cup mayonnaise or plain Greek yogurt

⅓ cup fresh cilantro leaves

1 jalapeño chile, stemmed and cut into chunks

2 tablespoons grated fresh gingerroot

2 tablespoons fresh lime juice

2 cloves garlic, halved

1 teaspoon grated lime zest

Heat oven to 400 degrees. Line 2 large rimmed baking sheets with foil. Place the almonds and sesame seeds in the bowl of a food processor fit with the metal blade. Process until coarsely chopped. Add the cornflakes, salt, and red pepper; process until finely chopped. Pour mixture into a shallow dish.

Place the flour in a second shallow dish, then lightly beat the eggs with ¼ cup water in a third dish. Lightly dredge the mushroom pieces in the flour, dip them into the eggs, then roll them in the cornflake coating. Place them on the baking sheets and drizzle with the oil. Bake for 15 to 20 minutes or until crisp and golden brown.

Meanwhile, place all the dip ingredients in the food processor. Blend until smooth and serve with the mushroom chunks.

kitchen notes

You could shallow-fry the coated mushrooms in an inch of peanut oil in a large cast-iron skillet for an even crunchier finish, but the oven method gives you a little time to zip up the dipping sauce and have the bites ready at the same time. I like firm chicken of the woods or mildly flavored puffballs served this way; for either mushroom you'll likely have a generous find that will give you plenty to work with.

cream of mushroom & root vegetable soup

serves 6

¼ cup (¼ ounce) dried king bolete mushrooms

olive oil

1 cup chopped shallot

1 cup chopped rutabaga (Swede)

½ cup chopped parsnip or carrot

coarse salt and freshly ground pepper to taste

¾ pound fresh shaggy mane and/or lobster mushrooms, trimmed and thinly sliced

3 cloves garlic, finely chopped

4 cups chicken, mushroom (see page 292), or vegetable stock

1 cup dry sherry

1 tablespoon fresh thyme leaves

½ cup heavy cream

Cover the dried mushrooms with warm tap water; let soak for 20 minutes. Scoop the mushrooms from the soaking liquid; chop. Strain the liquid through a double-folded piece of cheesecloth or a coffee filter; set aside.

Heat 2 tablespoons oil in a Dutch oven or large soup kettle over medium-high heat. Add the shallot, rutabaga, and parsnip to pan; season with salt and pepper. Sauté about 8 minutes. Add the fresh mushrooms, along with the soaked mushrooms and the garlic. Sauté about 8 minutes, then stir in the strained soaking liquid. Cook until all the moisture is evaporated and the vegetables start to brown.

Pour in the stock and sherry; add the thyme. Simmer for 20 minutes. Using an immersion blender, process the soup until smooth (or carefully process the hot soup in a blender). Stir in the cream and simmer for another minute or until heated through. Season to taste with salt and pepper.

kitchen notes

If you'd like a pretty final finish for a more formal presentation, save out some of the fresh mushrooms to sauté separately in a bit of butter. Swirl a spoonful of tangy crème fraîche into each bowl, spoon some mushrooms on top, and sprinkle with a few fresh thyme leaves.

Wild mushrooms, shaggy manes in particular, really stand out in a creamy soup. If you've got a nice harvest of shaggies, be sure to use them right away.

smoked chicken with smoky mushroom panzanella

serves 8

2 (3½–pound) whole chickens

coarse salt

1½ pounds fresh king boletes and/or hen of the woods mushrooms

olive oil

freshly ground pepper to taste

¾ pound crusty country-style bread, torn into 1½–inch pieces (6 cups)

2 medium fennel bulbs, cored and chopped (save some of the fronds)

1 medium red onion, chopped

6 large cloves garlic, thinly sliced

⅓ cup chicken broth

¼ cup sherry vinegar (or a combination of cider and balsamic vinegar)

2 tablespoons chopped fresh rosemary, sage, lavender, and/or thyme

8 cups torn mixed fresh salad greens (arugula, baby mustard greens, radicchio, endive)

sliced end-of-summer tomatoes, if you'd like

Tie the chicken legs with twine and tuck the wings under; liberally rub each chicken with 1½ tablespoons salt, concentrating on the thicker parts of the birds (don't worry about seasoning inside very much—just a sprinkle of salt). Place on a rimmed baking sheet and refrigerate, uncovered, for several hours or up to overnight.

If the mushrooms are large, cut them in half or quarters or tear them into large pieces. Drizzle them with oil and season well with salt and pepper; refrigerate with the chicken.

Heat your smoker according to the manufacturer's directions. Wipe the chickens dry and rub well with some oil. Place them on the top rack of the smoker. Arrange the mushrooms on trays or foil pans that will fit on the lower racks in your smoker.

Smoke the mushrooms for about 1 hour. Coarsely chop and transfer them to a parchment-lined baking sheet; cover and refrigerate. Continue smoking the chickens for about 4 hours (at 225 to 250 degrees) or until no longer pink near the thigh bones and the juices run clear (165 degrees internal temperature on an instant-read thermometer). The chickens should be a mahogany brown, with crisp skin.

Meanwhile, about an hour before the chicken is done, heat oven to 375 degrees. Toss the bread with ¼ cup oil on a large rimmed baking sheet; spread out into a single layer. Remove the tray of mushrooms from the fridge. Place both pans in the oven and toast the bread and roast the mushrooms for 15 to 20 minutes or until golden brown and crisp. Remove from the oven and let cool. Pour the bread and mushrooms into a large bowl. Set aside.

Heat 2 tablespoons oil in a large heavy skillet over medium-high heat. Sauté the fennel, onion, and garlic for about 6 minutes or until softened. Stir in broth and vinegar. Season with the fresh herbs, salt, and pepper; spoon over the toasted bread and mushrooms and toss everything together.

Arrange greens and tomatoes on a large serving platter; spoon the bread salad on top. Carve the chickens to serve.

kitchen notes
Many hunters who smoke birds, from grouse (as seen in our photo), pheasants, and ducks to wild turkey, will use a wet

(Continued on page 240)

brine to ensure the meat won't dry out during a long, slow cooking. But domestic chickens aren't as lean, and I think it's easier to dry brine them. A generous rub of coarse salt and good chilling for several hours works well and takes you to the same place: a platter of juicy chicken.

If you don't have an official smoker, turn your grill into one: Build an indirect fire or turn on only half of your gas grill. Soak a fair amount of wood chunks—applewood or cherrywood is nice—then add them to the hot coals or pile them in a foil pan under the grill rack. Let them smolder as you cook both the chickens and the mushrooms. The timing will be different—a smoker unit keeps the heat quite low—but the flavor and aroma will still be there.

· · · · ·

pan-grilled porcini steaks with bagna cauda butter
serves 4

½ cup (4 ounces) unsalted butter, softened

5 oil-packed anchovies, finely chopped

2 large cloves garlic, finely chopped

⅓ cup finely chopped fresh parsley

1 tablespoon olive oil

8 large fresh king bolete (porcini) mushrooms, trimmed and cut vertically into ½-inch slices

coarse salt and freshly ground pepper or grains of paradise to taste

toasted slices of crusty bread, if you'd like

Mix the butter, anchovies, half the garlic, and 2 tablespoons parsley together until well blended; set aside. Mix the remaining garlic with the remaining parsley; set aside.

Heat the oil in a heavy grill pan over medium-high heat. Place the mushrooms in the pan; season with salt and pepper. Sear both sides of mushrooms; add small spoonfuls of the seasoned butter to the pan. Cook until the mushrooms are tender and golden brown.

Serve mushroom slices with remaining butter, sprinkled with parsley on toasted bread.

kitchen notes
If you've got any Compound Wild Mushroom Herb Butter (see page 289) on hand you could use that instead, adding a smear of anchovy paste. Intensely flavored salted anchovies are high in the same naturally occurring glutamates that mushrooms contain, imbuing dishes with a rounded undertone that, when used in small amounts, makes most people want to eat more. If you make croûtes, lightly brush with olive oil and toast in a hot skillet or in the oven, then rub with a cut clove of raw garlic.

chicken marsala with porcini mushrooms & roasted grapes

serves 4

2 medium heads garlic

½ pound fresh king bolete (porcini) mushrooms, trimmed and sliced

1½ cups seedless red grapes, broken into small clusters

2 tablespoons olive oil

coarse salt and freshly ground pepper to taste

1 cup dry Marsala wine, divided

1 pound boneless, skinless chicken breast halves

2 tablespoons butter

3 tablespoons nonpareil capers or 12 large caper berries with stems

Heat oven to 400 degrees. Break the garlic heads into cloves, then peel each one. Toss in a large ovenproof skillet or pan with the mushrooms, grapes, and oil. Season with salt and pepper.

Place the skillet on the stovetop over medium heat for about 2 minutes; stir in ½ cup wine. Transfer to the oven and roast for 25 to 30 minutes, stirring occasionally, until the mushrooms and grapes are very tender and the garlic is golden brown.

Meanwhile, place the chicken between two pieces of plastic; flatten the chicken to ¼-inch thickness with a rolling pin or the flat side of a meat mallet. Season with salt and pepper.

Heat the butter in a second large skillet over medium-high heat. Add the chicken; sauté about 6 minutes, turning once, or until browned and no longer pink in the center. Add the capers to the skillet; cook and stir for 1 minute. Pour in the remaining ½ cup wine; reduce heat and simmer for 5 minutes.

Serve the chicken with the pan juices, topped with the grapes, mushrooms, and garlic.

kitchen notes

There's a reason that versions of chicken or veal cutlets quickly cooked with sweetly fortified Marsala wine are entertaining standards—and this rendition, with autumn king boletes and harvest grapes, is pretty classy. For a lightly thickened sauce, dredge the pounded chicken in seasoned flour before sautéing it. And here's a kitchen trick: Place the garlic cloves in a medium metal bowl, then turn over a second bowl of the same size on top. Holding the edges of the bowls together, shake them hard—the garlic will clank about like crazy—and magically the papery skins will rub off the cloves within a minute or so.

tea-smoked mushrooms & hmong glass noodles

serves 4

for the mushrooms
¾ pound fresh small king boletes, halved, or torn chicken of the woods or hen of the woods mushrooms

¼ cup soy sauce

2 tablespoons rice vinegar

¼ cup honey

1 tablespoon grated fresh gingerroot

2 cloves garlic, crushed

¼ cup sugar

¼ cup jasmine, green, or lapsang souchong tea leaves

2 cloves star anise

¼ teaspoon coriander seed

¼ cup jasmine rice

for the noodles
4 ounces uncooked cellophane or bean thread (glass) noodles

2 tablespoons rice vinegar

2 tablespoons fresh lime juice

1 tablespoon plus 1½ teaspoons fish sauce

2 teaspoons sambal oelek (garlic-chili sauce)

1 teaspoon honey

½ cup matchstick-cut carrot

½ cup matchstick-cut red bell pepper

¼ cup thinly sliced shallots

fresh cilantro and Thai basil leaves to taste

chopped dry-roasted peanuts

Place a large metal or bamboo steamer basket in a 12-inch wok with 1 inch of water in the bottom. Place the mushrooms in the basket. Cover and steam over high heat for 5 minutes.

Remove basket from wok and pour out the water. Place the mushrooms in a large bowl; mix in the soy sauce, 2 tablespoons rice vinegar, ¼ cup honey, ginger, and garlic. Let the mushrooms marinate for 30 minutes. Lift them from the marinade and pat dry; discard the marinade.

Meanwhile, line the inside of the wok with heavy-duty foil, extending it 5 inches over each end. Add the sugar, tea, star anise, coriander, and rice; stir until well mixed.

Place the wok over medium-high heat; cook for 5 minutes or until the mixture begins to smoke. Place the mushrooms back in the steamer basket and set inside wok. Place another sheet of foil over the mushrooms and fold the overhanging foil up and around the basket; crimp the foil to seal the edges to keep the smoke inside. Cook over medium heat for 15 minutes, then remove from heat and allow the mushrooms to smoke for 20 minutes longer.

To make the noodles, place the uncooked bean threads in a large bowl. Cover with very hot tap water; let stand for 15 minutes, until softened.

Mix the 2 tablespoons rice vinegar, lime juice, fish sauce, garlic-chili sauce, and 1 teaspoon honey in a small bowl. Drain the noodles well. Stir in the carrot, bell pepper, and shallots; toss with the dressing.

(Continued on page 244)

Unwrap the mushrooms and coarsely chop. Serve the noodles topped with the mushrooms, handfuls of torn fresh herbs, and peanuts.

kitchen notes

Smoking foods indoors has a long history, from converting woks into smokers in China to using small dishes of smoldering charcoal inside covered casseroles of food in India. The first time I jerry-rigged a stovetop smoker I was worried it would be a repeat of using an oven plank, which filled my house with an invasive smoky aroma that took days to dissipate. But mushrooms don't need much time to absorb the smokiness, and it's a fun process in the dead of winter when mushrooming and grilling are but a daydream. If you experiment with Lapsang souchong tea, know that it's already been smoked over pinewood, so it will create very potent smoke—which may be more intense and overpowering than you might like.

· · · · ·

sumac-rubbed venison with mostarda of fall fruits

serves 4

for the mostarda

1 cup honey

½ cup cider vinegar

2 tablespoons ground mustard

2 firm pears, chopped

1 cup fresh or frozen cranberries

½ cup mixed dried fruit (apricots, cherries, currants)

2 tablespoons grated fresh gingerroot

1 tablespoon mustard seed, if you'd like more bite

pomegranate arils (seeds), if you'd like

To make the mostarda, mix the honey and vinegar with 2 cups water in a large saucepan over medium-high heat. Whisk in the mustard until well blended. Stir in the pears, cranberries, dried fruit, and ginger. Bring to a boil; reduce heat and simmer about 45 minutes or until the fruit is tender and the mixture is thickened. Cool; stir in mustard seed and pomegranate seeds.

Meanwhile, mix the sumac, fennel, pepper, and salt in a small bowl. Rub the mixture over both sides of the venison steaks.

Heat 1 tablespoon oil and butter in a heavy skillet over medium-high heat. Add the steaks; cook for 4 to 6 minutes, turning once, for medium rare. Remove to a warm plate and tent with foil.

Add 1 tablespoon oil to the pan. Sauté the mushrooms for 8 to 10 minutes, stirring frequently, until they release their juices and are tender and well browned. Season with salt and pepper. Stir in mustard greens.

for the meat & mushrooms

1 tablespoon ground sumac

½ teaspoon fennel seed, crushed

½ teaspoon freshly ground black peppercorns or crushed grains of paradise

coarse salt to taste

1½ pounds venison or elk loin, cut into 4 thick steaks, or 4 center-cut pork chops

olive oil

1 tablespoon butter

½ pound mixed fresh wild mushrooms (black trumpet, king bolete, hen of the woods), trimmed and sliced or torn

3 cups torn young mustard greens

Serve the steaks on a bed of the mushrooms and greens, with a bowl of mostarda to pass around the table.

kitchen notes

Mushrooms are considered fruitings, so I'm inviting them to be part of the fall fruit family. I like how they meld with a condiment like mostarda and the richness of game meat—all have an underlying sweetness. A *mostarda* is a northern Italian sweet-and-sour simmered fruit sauce—reminiscent of chutney—traditionally served with boiled meats. It makes the most of fall fruits, both fresh and dried, and if made authentically will take you several days. This method celebrates what is easily found around here—pears or tart apples, plums, wild grapes, or the cranberries that flourish in bogs in western Wisconsin.

Brilliant red berry cones (called drupes or sumac bobs) weigh down the branches of sumac, a wild bush that grows along roadsides (the nontoxic kind, naturally: poison sumac has white berries). The rusty red leaves are the first to turn in the fall, a sure sign that the weather is growing cooler. You can harvest your own berries and make tea or this tangy condiment. For the sumac powder, just dry a batch of berries, either on a tray in the open air, in a dehydrator, or even in the microwave on low power (and I may toss in a handful of juniper berries I gather in my yard), then buzz them in a spice grinder (be sure to shake them in a fine sieve afterward to separate the fruit from bits of twig and seeds). Or look for little tins of the rosy powder at a Mediterranean or Middle Eastern market. The ground powder lends a tartness to a combo of other spices that works well with game meats.

The grains of paradise might be a treasure hunt, but if you find some you'll be rewarded with a lingering slow burn that is pepperlike, but more floral and spiced. Mix some with black peppercorns in a grinder for a full, sweet spiciness every time you season a panful of mushrooms.

maple & spice duck breasts with oven-charred cèpes & baby carrots

serves 4

2 tablespoons maple sugar

¾ teaspoon smoked paprika

1 teaspoon crushed coriander seed

¼ teaspoon freshly ground smoked salt

3 dried juniper berries, coarsely ground

4 boneless, skin-on duck breast halves

olive oil

12 baby carrots with tops, trimmed and halved lengthwise

¾ pound fresh king bolete (cèpe) mushrooms, whole if small or thickly sliced if larger

coarse salt and freshly ground pepper to taste

maple syrup, if you'd like

Heat oven to 425 degrees. Arrange the oven racks so you can slide in 2 baking sheets and a skillet. Mix the maple sugar, paprika, coriander, smoked salt, and juniper berries. Rub the duck with 1 tablespoon oil, then sprinkle on the seasoning blend.

Arrange carrots on a parchment-lined rimmed baking sheet. Spread mushrooms out on a second baking sheet. Drizzle carrots and mushrooms with 2 tablespoons oil; season with salt and pepper. Place pans in oven; roast for about 30 minutes or until tender and slightly charred around the edges.

Meanwhile, heat 1 tablespoon oil in a heavy ovenproof skillet over medium-high heat. Sear the duck, giving it a nice golden color. Slip the skillet into the oven; roast for 10 minutes or until desired doneness.

Serve the duck, sliced, with the roasted mushrooms and carrots. Drizzle with a little maple syrup.

kitchen notes

Cèpe is the French word for king boletes—and they're as much a fall favorite in France as they are in Italy (*porcini*) or here. Duck breasts are wonderful with the sweet-spicy combination of maple and spices, sliced up medium-rare, with the richness of the mushrooms and natural sweetness of the roasted carrots.

Meaty duck breasts are called *magret* in France, from the ducks grown to produce foie gras. The breasts are large and are most often quickly seared with the skin on in a super-hot skillet, then sliced and served rare like steak. I learned this classic technique in cooking school, then found myself married to a bird hunter. The duck breasts I'm lucky enough to get now are wild, boned out of much smaller birds, already skinned, and accompanied with a reminder to be watchful for shot with each bite. The flavor of untamed birds is a perfect match for untamed mushrooms, each vying for attention on the plate but very happy partners all the same.

Be sure to use a good maple syrup: I love the gorgeous amber syrup produced by our friend Todd Overland at his family sugar shack in northern Minnesota, under the label Muddy Foot Prints.

maitake mousse

serves 4 to 6

5 tablespoons butter, divided

½ pound fresh hen of the woods (maitake) mushrooms, torn into small pieces

⅔ cup chopped shallot

2 cloves garlic, finely chopped

coarse salt and freshly ground pepper to taste

½ cup mascarpone cheese, crumbled fresh goat cheese, or plain whipped cream cheese

1 tablespoon fresh marjoram or thyme leaves

½ cup heavy cream, softly whipped

crisp rye flatbread crackers

flavored balsamic vinegar (cranberry walnut, blackberry ginger, fig)

Melt 3 tablespoons butter in a large skillet over medium-high heat. Sauté the mushrooms for about 8 minutes or until tender and crisply brown around the edges. Scrape into the bowl of a food processor fit with the metal blade. Melt the remaining 2 tablespoons butter in the skillet over medium heat. Sauté the shallot and garlic for 4 minutes or until translucent. Scrape into the food processor with the mushrooms.

Process the mushroom mixture until very smooth; season with salt and pepper. Add the mascarpone and marjoram to the food processor. Process just until blended. Scrape the mixture into a medium bowl, then fold in the cream.

Spoon the mousse into a ramekin and chill for at least 1 hour. Serve spread on crisp flatbread with a little drizzle of balsamic vinegar.

kitchen notes

I tasted a similar mousse at a private club one early autumn and was intrigued by how simply delicious it was. The server divulged that the mushrooms were foraged by a groundskeeper at a golf course just across the road from my house. I spent the rest of that fall walking along the edges of the course, inspecting the base of every oak I saw. I never had any luck: I'm sure I'll always lose the race to someone who walks the terrain every day. A lesson in diligent searching if you want hunting success.

iron ranger pasties

serves 4

1 cup unbleached all-purpose flour

¾ cup rye flour

¼ cup cornmeal

1 teaspoon fine salt

14 tablespoons cold butter, cut into small chunks

½ cup ice water

2 tablespoons bacon fat or butter

¼ cup finely chopped onion

2 cups finely chopped mixed fresh wild mushrooms (giant puffball, chanterelle, hen of the woods, king bolete)

½ cup diced (¼-inch) russet potato

½ cup diced (¼-inch) rutabaga (Swede)

2 tablespoons chopped fresh marjoram

coarse salt and freshly ground pepper to taste

1 egg, lightly beaten

brown mustard, if you'd like

To make the pastry dough, place the flours, cornmeal, and salt in the bowl of a food processor fit with the metal blade. Add the butter and pulse the blade until the mixture is like a coarse meal. Sprinkle in the ice water; process just until the dough starts to come together—you should still see some bits of butter. Scrape the dough out onto a work surface. Gather it gently into a ball and cut it into 4 pieces. Form each piece into a flat ½-inch-thick disk and wrap in plastic or waxed paper. Refrigerate for at least 1 hour, until chilled and firm.

Heat oven to 425 degrees. Melt the bacon fat in a medium skillet over medium-high heat. Sauté the onion and mushrooms for about 6 minutes or until the mushrooms release their juices. Continue cooking until all the liquid is evaporated. Add the potato and rutabaga to the skillet and mix well; stir in the marjoram and season well with salt and pepper. Let the mixture cool while you roll out the pastry.

Take the pastry rounds from the fridge. I like to use a silicone baking mat, but you could just flour your work surface or a pastry cloth to roll out the dough into 6- to 7-inch rounds. Divide the vegetable mixture between the pastry rounds, spooning it onto half of each circle. Brush the edges with some egg. Fold the dough over the filling, creating large half-moons. Crimp the edges together so the pasties are well sealed—use the tines of a fork or crimp with your fingers like the edge of a pie.

Place the pasties on a large parchment-lined baking pan and brush with the remaining egg wash. Bake for about 45 minutes or until golden brown. Serve hot or at room temperature, with some brown mustard on the side.

kitchen notes

Pronounced "pass-tee," these hand pies have roots in the Iron Range of north-central Minnesota and the Upper Peninsula of Michigan—a New World continuation of a tradition from the coal mines in Cornwall, England. I've heard them called Iron Range comfort food. Hefty, hand-formed crescents, these on-the-go meat pot pies were a simple, portable lunch for miners. During the height of the mining industry, local bakers marked each miner's initials on his pasty. The thick pastry, often made with suet, was tough enough to withstand being dropped down a mine shaft and, wrapped in a towel, could stay warm for hours. You can still find bakeries on the Iron Range and in the UP that keep the tradition alive.

winter solstice

craft beer–braised pot roast

serves 8

1 cup (1 ounce) dried king bolete mushrooms or a blend of dried mushrooms

1 (4- to 5-pound) boneless beef chuck roast or bone-in pork shoulder roast

coarse salt and freshly ground pepper to taste

2 tablespoons instant dark-roast coffee

1 tablespoon fennel seed, divided

olive oil

2 large onions, sliced

4 cloves garlic, peeled and halved

1 cup pitted prunes

1 teaspoon dried thyme leaves, crushed

1 teaspoon dried oregano leaves, crushed

1 (12-ounce) bottle porter or dark amber beer

2 tablespoons unbleached all-purpose flour

2 tablespoons butter, softened

torn fresh herbs (oregano, thyme, parsley), if you'd like

Cover the mushrooms with warm tap water; let stand while you brown the meat, about 20 minutes or until plumped and softened.

Heat oven to 350 degrees. Season the roast well with salt, pepper, the ground coffee, and about 1 teaspoon fennel seeds. Heat a small splash of oil in a large Dutch oven or braising pan over medium-high heat. Sear the meat on all sides, taking your time, until the roast is well browned. Transfer the roast to a tray.

Heat a little more oil in the pan. Add the onions and garlic; sauté for about 10 minutes or until tender and starting to color. Stir in the prunes, remaining fennel seeds, thyme, and oregano. Return the roast and any juices to the pan.

Scoop out the mushrooms and pour soaking liquid through double-folded cheesecloth or a coffee filter. Add the mushrooms and liquid to the pan, along with the beer. Bring to a simmer, cover, and place in the oven for about 3 hours or until the roast is very tender.

Transfer the roast to a serving platter. Mash the flour and butter together. Season the cooking liquid and vegetables with salt and pepper, then whisk in the flour paste. Simmer until the sauce is thickened. Serve spooned over large chunks of the roast. Sprinkle with fresh herbs.

kitchen notes

Playing with savory and sweet is flavor warping: rich meat and earthy mushrooms, roasted malty beer with an edge of coffee, sweet fennel and prunes, and a final spike of bright herbal high notes. It all reminds me of a good brisket and Sunday suppers. As a kid, I regularly filled up on too much black licorice candy at the cinema, then couldn't wait for that Sunday pot roast, slowly braising in the oven while we were away. I'm pretty sure my mom didn't use a small-batch artisan brew, but she most definitely embraced a bracing shot of dry sherry in her pot roasts, along with a few cupfuls of fresh mushrooms. The intense flavor of dried mushrooms only makes things better.

Slow-roast a couple of bunches of baby carrots with trimmed tops to serve alongside, with a big bowl of mashed parsnips or garlicky smashed potatoes.

kielbasa & sauerkraut soup

serves 8

2 cups (2 ounces) dried wild mushrooms (king bolete or lobster)

½ pound smoked kielbasa

2 tablespoons olive oil

1½ cups chopped onion

2 cups diced (¼-inch) carrot

¾ cup diced (¼-inch) celery

2 cloves garlic, finely chopped

2 cups shredded cabbage

4 cups diced (½-inch) russet potato

1½ teaspoons caraway seed, toasted and crushed

1½ teaspoons smoked paprika

¼ teaspoon dill seed

coarse salt and freshly ground pepper to taste

6–7 cups good-quality low-sodium chicken broth

2 cups sauerkraut, rinsed and drained

sour cream and torn fresh dill, if you'd like

Cover the mushrooms with warm tap water; let stand for 30 minutes or until plumped and softened. Scoop out the mushrooms and coarsely chop. Strain the soaking liquid through a double-folded piece of cheesecloth or a coffee filter; set aside.

Heat a large soup kettle or Dutch oven over medium-high heat. Cut the sausage in half lengthwise, then cut crosswise into ¼-inch slices. Sauté in the hot pan for about 5 minutes or until browned. Transfer to a plate.

Heat the oil in the pan; sauté the onion, carrot, and celery for about 5 minutes. Stir in the garlic and continue cooking for another minute or two, until the vegetables are golden. Stir in the cabbage and mushrooms; cook and stir for about 2 minutes.

Add the potatoes, caraway, paprika, dill seed, salt, and pepper to the pan. Mix the reserved mushroom soaking liquid with enough chicken broth to equal 8 cups; pour into the pan. Cover and bring to a boil; uncover and reduce heat. Simmer for about 30 minutes or until the potatoes are tender. Stir in the sauerkraut. Serve the soup hot, with a spoonful of sour cream and a generous sprinkle of fresh dill.

kitchen notes

Kielbasa is the generic word for "sausage" in Polish—and can be so much more than what's in the grocery store bunker next to the hot dogs. If you can find a good Polish butcher, taste your way through the sausage case; I really like juniper sausage, which is semi-dry and smoked over juniper wood. The flavor of these various sausages is quite pronounced, so a lightly-smoked Polish frankfurter would meld well with the vegetables and dried mushrooms. Be sure to get a really good sauerkraut there, too. My Polish mushroom-loving friend John (see page 2) really wanted to give me his recipe for *bigos*—a hunter's stew filled with dried mushrooms, sausage, game meats, and sauerkraut. But his very Old World, undeniably extraordinary recipe takes three days to make.

smoked whitefish cakes with horseradish mushroom compote

serves 4

1½ cups flaked smoked whitefish

2 tablespoons chopped green onion

2 teaspoons grated lemon zest

coarse salt and freshly ground pepper to taste

1 large egg, lightly beaten

¼ cup heavy cream

1½ cups fresh multigrain bread crumbs, divided

olive oil

½ cup finely chopped onion

½ pound fresh king bolete mushrooms, sliced

¼ cup dry white wine

3 cups Roasted Wild Mushroom Stock (see page 292) or vegetable stock

1 tablespoon unbleached all-purpose flour dissolved in 2 tablespoons water

1 tablespoon butter

1–2 tablespoons freshly grated horseradish root

fresh thyme leaves to taste

Mix whitefish, green onion, lemon zest, salt, and pepper in a medium bowl. Stir in egg, cream, and ½ cup bread crumbs. Form mixture into 8 (½-inch) patties using a ¼-cup measure.

Spread the remaining 1 cup bread crumbs on a plate; coat fish cakes. Heat 2 tablespoons oil in a large heavy skillet over medium heat. Cook the fish patties in batches for about 6 minutes, turning once, until golden brown. Add more oil as needed. Transfer the fish cakes to a serving platter; cover with foil (keep warm in a low oven).

To make the compote, heat 1 tablespoon oil in the skillet over medium-high heat. Add the onion; sauté for 1 minute. Stir in mushrooms; season with salt and pepper. Sauté for about 8 minutes or until they release their juices and begin to brown. Stir in the wine; cook until evaporated. Stir the stock into the skillet and simmer for 10 minutes or until reduced by half. Whisk in the flour slurry; bring to a boil. Reduce heat to low and simmer until slightly thickened. Remove from heat; stir in the butter and horseradish. Serve the fish cakes topped with mushroom compote, sprinkled with thyme.

kitchen notes

Our neighbor up at our lake place in northern Minnesota, Gary Brumberg, is a single-minded fisherman and hunter. He lives by the seasons, including netting whitefish in the late fall, and he loves to share recipes. This is a take on his fish cakes, a North Shore version of ground fish patties that are beloved by anglers anywhere near a lake.

wild rice & hen–stuffed cabbage leaves

serves 8

1 large head cabbage (you'll want 20 large green cabbage leaves)

6 tablespoons butter, divided

1½ cups chopped onion

4 cloves garlic, finely chopped

2 cups chopped fresh hen of the woods mushrooms

1 pound ground grass-fed beef

½ pound ground pork

2 eggs

2 cups wild rice, cooked until the kernels pop

2 teaspoons rubbed dried sage

½ cup chopped fresh parsley

coarse salt and freshly ground pepper to taste

warm crushed tomatoes, seasoned with a bit of fresh rosemary, if you'd like

Bring a large stockpot of water to a boil. Core the cabbage and submerge it into the boiling water for 2 minutes. Lift the cabbage out and peel off as many leaves as you can. Lay them out on a tray. Repeat dipping the cabbage and peeling off leaves until you have what you need (if some of the leaves are small you may need 2 to make a stuffed roll—and you can trim the rib down the larger leaves so they're easier to roll). Chop up whatever cabbage is left; set aside.

Melt 2 tablespoons butter in a large heavy skillet over medium-high heat. Add the onion and garlic; sauté for 5 minutes. Stir in the mushrooms; sauté for about 6 minutes or until tender.

Place the beef and pork in a large bowl. Gently mix in the sautéed vegetables with your hands. Mix in the eggs, wild rice, sage, parsley, and plenty of salt and pepper.

Heat oven to 350 degrees. Butter a 3-quart (13x9–inch) baking dish and spread the chopped cabbage evenly over the bottom. Taking one leaf at a time, place about ¼ cup of the stuffing in the center and wrap it up, tucking in the sides to make a little package. Repeat with the rest of the leaves and filling.

Melt the remaining 4 tablespoons butter in the skillet over medium-high heat; brown the rolls and arrange in the baking dish. Cover with foil. Bake for 45 minutes or until the rolls are cooked through. Serve with a spoonful of crushed tomatoes.

kitchen notes

Pegi Lee is my truly amazing cooking inspiration. Peg is devoted not only to her Norwegian roots, making traditional lefse every year on her vintage lefse griddle, but to making wonderful whole foods from scratch every day. She gardens, forages, and preserves everything imaginable. I can only aspire to her energy. She shared her version of stuffed cabbage rolls, filled with hand-harvested wild rice and hen of the woods mushrooms. If it's too late to find fresh, you can buy cultivated maitake or rehydrate some dried hens, king boletes, or lobsters with a few black trumpets thrown in. To dry hens, Peg likes to pull them apart, lay them out on a rack over a sheet pan, and fan dry them. She freezes them in layers separated by waxed paper. Peg suggests coring, blanching, then freezing the head of cabbage for a little while to make peeling the leaves easier.

butcher's best beef stroganoff

serves 6 to 8

1½ cups (1½ ounces) dried king bolete or lobster mushrooms

beef broth

1 cup unbleached all-purpose flour

coarse salt and freshly ground pepper to taste

2 pounds lean stew beef, cut into chunks

½ cup (4 ounces) butter

1 cup chopped onion

½ cup tomato juice

½ cup dry sherry or hearty Burgundy wine

1 cup sour cream

hot cooked rice or buttered egg noodles

Cover the dried mushrooms with warm tap water; let stand for about 30 minutes or until plumped and softened. Scoop out the mushrooms, squeezing out excess water; coarsely chop mushrooms. Strain the soaking liquid through double-folded cheesecloth or a coffee filter. Pour into a 2-cup measure, adding enough beef broth so you have 2 cups of liquid. Set aside.

Heat oven to 350 degrees. Place the flour in a shallow dish and season it well with salt and pepper. Dredge the beef in the flour until heavily coated.

Melt the butter in a large Dutch oven or covered casserole over medium-high heat. Add the beef chunks and brown them well. Add the onions and mushrooms; cook and stir for another few minutes. Stir in the tomato juice, mushroom-beef broth, sherry, and sour cream. Cover the pan and place in the oven.

Bake the stroganoff for 2 to 2½ hours, stirring occasionally, until the beef is tender and the sauce is thick. Serve spooned over rice or noodles.

kitchen notes

If you still have some fresh king boletes or hen of the woods at the end of the season, use them instead of dried boletes. Slice up about a half pound of fresh mushrooms and sauté them with the onions. You could even enrich the sauce with a spoonful of powdered king boletes.

This adaptation comes from my aunt Janet and uncle Charlie's tried-and-true family recipe. Uncle Charlie was a butcher who would fill the back of our Country Squire station wagon with cooler boxes full of beef each fall; my siblings and I would lie on top of the boxes (nary a seatbelt in sight) for the long drive home. We kids always knew that company was coming if the aroma of stroganoff wafted through the house on Sunday; dinner would be served over baked rice with a fancy hot bacon-spinach salad.

porcini-dusted chicken with wild mushroom farrotto

serves 4

2 cups (2 ounces) dried king bolete (porcini) mushrooms

4 bone-in split chicken breasts (2 pounds total)

olive oil

coarse salt and freshly ground pepper to taste

½ cup chopped shallots

1 cup uncooked farro

½ cup dry white wine

2½ cups chicken broth or stock

chopped fresh sage or rosemary and freshly grated Reggiano-Parmigiano cheese, if you'd like

Heat oven to 400 degrees. Put 1½ cups dried mushrooms in a medium bowl; pour in 2 cups warm water and let stand for 20 to 30 minutes or until tender. Place the remaining mushrooms in a spice or clean coffee grinder; process until finely ground. Lightly rub the chicken with a little olive oil and season with salt and pepper. Sprinkle both sides of each breast with the mushroom powder. Place in a lightly greased baking dish. Bake about 30 minutes or until no longer pink near bone. Cover with foil and keep warm until the farro is done.

Meanwhile, scoop the soaked mushrooms out of the water, squeezing them gently to remove as much water as possible. Coarsely chop them and set aside. Strain the soaking liquid through a double-folded piece of cheesecloth or a coffee filter; set aside.

Heat 1 tablespoon oil in a small Dutch oven or large saucepan over medium-high heat. Sauté the shallots about 3 minutes or until tender, stirring frequently. Add mushrooms; cook about 4 minutes.

Stir in the farro; cook 1 minute. Stir in wine; cook 1 minute or until wine evaporates. Reduce heat to medium. Add 1 cup of the strained mushroom liquid; cook 8 minutes or until liquid is nearly absorbed, stirring frequently. Repeat with 2 cups chicken broth, adding 1 cup at a time, stirring until absorbed (about 30 minutes total).

Stir the last ½ cup broth into the farro, cooking until heated through. Serve immediately with roasted chicken, finishing with a sprinkle of sage and some cheese.

kitchen notes

Porcini, what the Italians call king boletes, are traditional in a risotto made with Arborio or Carnaroli rice. But farro, or emmer, is one of a few varieties of ancient wheats that is quite common in northern Italy. Pearled farro doesn't take as long to cook as wheat or rye berries; its earthier flavor makes a fine choice in a creamy risotto with more bite. Using pulverized dried mushrooms to coat mildly flavored chicken breasts or whitefish fillets is a simple way to add a more robust taste in less than a moment in the kitchen. Porcini powder is quite aromatic and I think rather elegant.

mushroom & chestnut–stuffed pork chops

serves 4

6 cups torn bite-size pieces crusty country-style bread

2 cups (2 ounces) dried king bolete mushrooms (or, if you make this earlier in the fall, ½ pound fresh king bolete or hen of the woods mushrooms, trimmed and chopped)

4 tablespoons butter, divided

coarse salt and freshly ground pepper to taste

2 medium onions, chopped

4 stalks celery, chopped

1 tablespoon finely chopped fresh rosemary leaves

¾ pound vacuum-packed whole chestnuts, chopped (about 2 cups)

½ cup packed flat-leaf parsley sprigs, finely chopped

2 cups Roasted Wild Mushroom Stock (see page 292) or beef broth

4 double-cut (1-inch-thick) bone-in pork loin chops

1 tablespoon olive oil

Smoky Bacon Marmalade (at right), if you'd like, or a cranberry, apple, or pear chutney

Heat oven to 375 degrees. Spread the bread out on a rimmed baking sheet; toast for about 20 minutes or until a pale golden color. Transfer to a large bowl.

Cover the mushrooms with warm tap water; let soak for about 20 minutes. Scoop out mushrooms, squeezing out excess water; chop. Strain the soaking liquid through double-folded cheesecloth or a coffee filter; set aside.

Melt 1 tablespoon butter in a large ovenproof skillet over medium-high heat. Sauté the mushrooms for about 5 minutes or until they begin to brown. Season lightly with salt and pepper. Scrape into the bowl with the toasted bread.

Melt the remaining 3 tablespoons butter in the skillet. Sauté the onions, celery, and rosemary, stirring occasionally, for about 5 minutes or until softened. Add the chestnuts and cook, stirring, for 1 minute longer. Add to the bread mixture with the parsley; season with salt and pepper. Stir in the stock until everything is well moistened.

Using a sharp paring knife, cut a deep horizontal pocket into each pork chop. Spoon about ⅓ cup of the stuffing into each pocket; use a wooden pick to secure the filling. Season the chops well with salt and pepper. Spoon the remaining stuffing into a buttered baking dish.

Increase oven temperature to 425 degrees. Heat the oil in the skillet over high heat. Add the pork chops; sear them on both sides until nicely browned. Place the skillet and stuffing dish in the oven. Bake for about 20 minutes or until the chops are no longer pink and the dressing is hot and crispy on top. Serve with the bacon marmalade or a fruit chutney.

Smoky Bacon Marmalade: Chop 6 slices applewood-smoked bacon and cook until crispy in a large skillet. Remove bacon from pan, leaving fat. Cook 1 small onion, chopped, and 2 cloves garlic, finely chopped, in bacon fat over medium heat until softened. Stir in ⅓ cup packed brown sugar, ¼ cup apple cider vinegar, ¼ cup orange or cranberry juice, and 1 teaspoon chopped fresh rosemary. Bring to a boil; reduce heat and simmer for about 15 minutes or until syrupy. Remove from heat; stir in crisp bacon and a good grind of black pepper.

winterly mushroom & northern bean chili

serves 8

2 tablespoons olive oil

1 large onion, chopped

2 red (or any other color you like) bell peppers, chopped

3 cloves garlic, finely chopped

2 cups hen of the woods or chicken of the woods Freezer Wild Mushroom Duxelles (see page 284), thawed

coarse salt and freshly ground pepper to taste

2 (14.5-ounce) cans fire-roasted diced tomatoes, undrained

1 (14.5-ounce) can crushed tomatoes

2 chipotle chiles in adobo, chopped, plus some sauce to taste

1 (12-ounce) bottle amber ale or 1½ cups beef stock

1 tablespoon toasted cumin seed, crushed

1 tablespoon dried king bolete powder (see page 282)

2 teaspoons dried oregano leaves, crushed

1 teaspoon ground coriander

dash ground cinnamon

3 (15-ounce) cans great northern beans, rinsed and drained

torn fresh cilantro leaves

sour cream mixed with a bit of the adobo sauce and grated lime zest, if you'd like

chopped avocado, sliced green onions, fresh lime wedges

Heat the oil in a large Dutch oven or soup kettle over medium-high heat. Sauté the onion, bell peppers, and garlic for about 6 minutes or until softened. Add the thawed duxelles; cook and stir for about 3 minutes longer. Season with salt and pepper.

Stir in the diced and crushed tomatoes, along with the chipotle chile and enough of the adobo sauce for the level of heat you like. Stir in the beer, cumin, mushroom powder, oregano, coriander, and cinnamon. Simmer the chili, uncovered, for about 20 minutes or until thick.

Stir in the beans and simmer until heated through. Serve chili topped with a shower of cilantro and a swirl of flavored sour cream. Set out little dishes of avocado, green onion, and limes.

kitchen notes

The texture of the duxelles adds an almost sausage-like bite, with a savory mushroomy boost from the intensity of the king bolete powder. If you plant your own dry ("shuckies" or shell) beans—such as great northern, cranberry, kidney, or pinto—after the last spring frost is past, you'll have your own stash of chili beans. Simmer them in unsalted mushroom or chicken stock until tender, then add to the pot. I really like a stack of warm white corn tortillas brushed with melted butter to eat on the side.

finnish split pea soup

serves 4 to 6

1 cup (1 ounce) dried chanterelle mushrooms (or 2 cups fresh late-season chanterelles)

1 tablespoon olive oil

1 large onion, chopped

2 large carrots or parsnips, peeled and chopped

3 stalks celery with some leaves, chopped

4 cloves garlic, finely chopped

1 pound dried green or yellow split peas, rinsed well

1 (1½–pound) smoked ham hock or smoked turkey drumstick, trimmed of excess fat

6 cups chicken broth

1 cup dry sherry

1 teaspoon dried thyme, crushed

1 teaspoon dried marjoram, crushed

¼ teaspoon ground allspice

lots of freshly ground pepper to taste

4 medium red or Yukon gold potatoes, cut into ½-inch cubes

3 cups torn fresh spinach leaves

Cover the dried mushrooms with warm tap water; let stand for 20 to 30 minutes or until plumped and softened. (If using fresh, chop and set aside.)

Meanwhile, heat the oil in a large Dutch oven or soup kettle over medium-high heat. Sauté the onion, carrots, celery, and garlic for about 5 minutes or until softened. Scoop the mushrooms out of the soaking water; squeeze to remove any excess water. Coarsely chop the mushrooms; add to the pan. Strain the soaking liquid through double-folded cheesecloth or coffee filter to remove any grit. Pour liquid into the vegetables.

Add the split peas, ham hock, broth, sherry, thyme, marjoram, allspice, and a hefty grind of pepper. Bring to a boil; reduce heat and simmer, partially covered, for about 3 hours or until split peas have fallen apart and soup is thickened. Stir soup occasionally to prevent it from sticking to the bottom of the pan.

When the soup is thick, stir in the potatoes and spinach; simmer for about 20 minutes or until potatoes are tender. Remove the ham hock (including any meat that's fallen off the bone) from the soup. Chop or shred the meat and stir back into the soup. Serve hot.

kitchen notes

A tradition in Finland is to eat pea soup, served with dark rye bread and a spoonful of mustard, on Thursdays. The meal is followed by oven-baked pancakes with strawberry jam.

Allspice, a pungently-flavored dried berry from the pimento tree that grows in Jamaica—and is sometimes called Jamaican pepper—is surprisingly popular in Finland. Sometimes substituted for black pepper, it adds a burst of spice that's like a blast of cloves, nutmeg, and cinnamon all rolled into one.

minced lemongrass mushroom–chicken lettuce wraps

serves 6 as an appetizer

for the mushroom-chicken filling

2 cups (2 ounces) mixed dried mushrooms (king bolete, lobster)

canola oil

2 tablespoons finely chopped lemongrass (use the more tender, fleshier inner part from the lower stalks)

2 cloves garlic, finely chopped

1 tablespoon grated fresh gingerroot

1 pound ground chicken

1 tablespoon tamari or soy sauce

1 tablespoon fish sauce

2 teaspoons toasted sesame oil

cracked black pepper to taste

⅓ cup sliced green onions

for the sauce

¾ cup hoisin sauce

3 tablespoons rice vinegar

3 tablespoons tamari or soy sauce

1 tablespoon plus 1½ teaspoons grated fresh gingerroot

1 tablespoon sambal oelek (chili-garlic sauce) or to taste

for serving

2 small heads butter or Bibb lettuce, broken into individual leaves

1 large bunch fresh cilantro, torn

1 large bunch fresh mint, torn

fresh lime wedges, if you'd like

Cover the mushrooms with warm tap water; let stand for 20 to 30 minutes or until plumped and softened. Scoop out the mushrooms, squeezing out any excess water. Finely chop them. Strain the soaking liquid through a double-folded piece of cheesecloth or a coffee filter.

Heat 1 tablespoon oil in a large skillet over medium-high heat. Sauté the lemongrass and garlic for 2 minutes. Stir in the mushrooms; sauté for 2 minutes, then pour in the mushroom soaking liquid. Bring to a boil, then reduce heat and continue cooking until all the liquid is nearly evaporated. Scrape the mushrooms into a bowl.

Heat 1 tablespoon oil in the skillet over medium heat. Sauté 1 tablespoon ginger for 1 minute. Break up the chicken into the pan; cook and stir for 6 to 8 minutes or until no longer pink. Stir in 1 tablespoon soy sauce, fish sauce, 2 teaspoons sesame oil, pepper, and green onions, along with the mushroom mixture.

Meanwhile, mix ingredients for the serving sauce in a small dish.

To serve, spoon the chicken-mushroom mixture into a bowl. Arrange the lettuce leaves on a plate or tray with the dish of dipping sauce. Each person can spoon some of the chicken and mushrooms into a lettuce leaf, generously topped with cilantro and mint, a spoonful of the sauce, and a squeeze of lime. Fold the lettuce over the filling and eat out of hand.

kitchen notes

If I'm short on time, tired, or lazy, I skip mixing up the formal sauce and just put out jars of hoisin and garlic chili sauce and a shaker bottle of tamari (which is generally less salty than soy sauce). The flavor of the minced mushrooms and ground chicken mixture is distinct but not overpowering, since pairing it with the fresh herb and condiment sauce adds up to such a big flavor hit. Though I call this out as an appetizer, it can be a fresh winter supper that brings an aura of summertime.

smoked trout & lobster chowder

serves 4

2 medium leeks

3 small carrots with tops

1 tablespoon olive oil

½ pound very small red potatoes, sliced

coarse salt and freshly ground pepper

2 cups (2 ounces) dried lobster mushrooms, rinsed well and chopped

2½ cups chicken or vegetable broth

1 (8-ounce) bottle clam juice

1 tablespoon fresh thyme leaves or 1 teaspoon dried thyme

½ pound smoked lake trout, flaked

3 cups half-and-half

sliced green onions

Trim the tough green tops from the leeks; toss into the compost bin. Cut leeks in half lengthwise and rinse out any sand. Trim carrot tops; set aside. Slice the leeks and carrots crosswise.

Heat oil in a Dutch oven or large soup kettle over medium-high heat. Add the leeks and carrots; sauté for 5 minutes. Add the potatoes to the pan; sauté for 5 minutes longer. Season with salt and pepper.

Add the mushrooms to the pan, then pour in the broth and clam juice. Stir in thyme. Bring to a boil; reduce heat to low and gently simmer, partially covered, about 30 minutes or until the vegetables are tender.

Stir in the smoked fish and half-and-half; gently simmer until heated through. Serve hot, sprinkled with green onions, chopped carrot tops, and freshly ground pepper.

kitchen notes

Add some chanterelle duxelles to the chowder if you have some in the freezer—they add a little different texture and rounder mushroom hit in the flavor department. This chowder is on the fancy side, well suited for company, though I'd still serve it with some nice saltine crackers.

last harvest hash

serves 4

½ cup (½ ounce) dried lobster or king bolete mushrooms

2 cups Yukon gold potatoes cut into ½-inch cubes

2 cups butternut or kabocha squash cut into ½-inch cubes

1½ cups peeled and chopped sunchokes (Jerusalem artichokes)

olive oil

1 large leek, halved lengthwise and rinsed well, then sliced crosswise

coarse salt and freshly ground pepper to taste

3 cups baby kale leaves

4 large eggs

¼ cup torn fresh sage and/or thyme leaves

hot pepper sauce to taste

Cover the mushrooms with warm tap water; let stand for about 20 minutes or until plumped and softened. Scoop out the mushrooms, squeezing any excess water back into the soaking liquid. Coarsely chop. Strain the soaking liquid through double-folded cheesecloth or a coffee filter. Set aside.

Meanwhile, place the potatoes, squash, and sunchokes in a steamer basket over an inch of water in a large pan. Steam the vegetables for about 15 minutes or until nearly tender. (Or micro-steam them in a glass bowl, adding about ¼ cup water, on high power for 4 minutes.)

Heat 1 tablespoon oil in a large heavy skillet over medium-high heat. Add the leeks; sauté for 2 minutes. Add the mushrooms and soaking liquid; cook and stir until the liquid is evaporated.

Add 2 tablespoons oil to the skillet; stir in the par-cooked potatoes, squash, and sunchokes. Season with salt and pepper. Sauté for about 5 minutes or until everything is tender. Stir the greens into the pan; cover and cook until wilted.

Make 4 wells in the center of the hash; crack an egg into each well. Reduce heat to medium and cook about 5 minutes or until the eggs are set. Sprinkle with fresh herbs and more salt and freshly ground pepper. Serve with hot sauce as desired.

kitchen notes
Sunchokes are a tuber that looks like a cousin to gingerroot but is no relation. Nor are they related to artichokes: they are actually from a family of sunflowers. Their nutty, slightly sweet flavor complements mushrooms and starchy vegetables. You can find them year 'round, but they're at their best when dug up after a light frost in the fall. If you've freshly harvested them, you might like to just keep their skin on, since they're small and have a bumpy surface. But if you'd prefer to take the skin off, use a vegetable peeler or rub off the skin after steaming or micro-cooking them.

madeira-braised mushroom chicken

serves 4

1½ cups (1½ ounces) dried king bolete mushrooms

8 bone-in chicken thighs (about 3 pounds total)

coarse salt and freshly ground pepper to taste

2 tablespoons olive oil

2 medium red onions, sliced

3 cloves garlic, finely chopped

¾ cup Madeira wine

2 tablespoons finely chopped fresh rosemary

2 tablespoons cornstarch dissolved in 3 tablespoons water

Place mushrooms in a medium bowl and cover with 2 cups warm tap water. Let them soak for 20 to 30 minutes or until plumped and softened. Scoop out the mushrooms; squeeze out any excess liquid. Strain the liquid through a double-folded piece of cheesecloth or a coffee filter. Set aside.

Heat oven to 350 degrees. Meanwhile, season the chicken with salt and pepper. Brown the pieces well in a large Dutch oven over medium-high heat. Transfer the chicken to a tray; remove the skin if you'd like (the fat from under the skin should already be rendered in the pan to flavor the stew).

Heat the oil in the pan; add the onions, garlic, and mushrooms. Cook and stir for 5 minutes or until softened. Return the chicken pieces to the pan. Pour the strained mushroom liquid and Madeira over the chicken and sprinkle with the rosemary.

Bring the mixture to a boil, then cover and place in the oven. Bake for 45 minutes or until the chicken is no longer pink near the bone.

Transfer the chicken to a serving platter with the onions and mushrooms. Whisk the dissolved cornstarch into the pan juices over medium-high heat. Cook and whisk until thickened. Spoon the sauce over the chicken.

kitchen notes

You can use a medium-dry Madeira or substitute Marsala or a richer style of dry sherry if you'd like; all are fortified wines with a rich nuttiness, but I think Madeira has a bit more personality. They all blend beautifully with the intensity of the dried mushrooms and the onions' light sweetness. I slowly braise the bone-in chicken thighs in a large pot in the oven, but buy yourself more time by using a slow cooker. Make a grainy pilaf like steamed bulgur or quinoa or mash some buttery potatoes—whatever you like to soak up the sauce.

janice's vegetable beef barley soup with salted mushroom-marrow toast

serves 8

3 (1½ inch–thick) beef shanks with meat (about 3 pounds total)

4 (¾ inch–thick) slices marrow bone (the shank without meat)

coarse salt

½ cup dry vermouth plus more to taste

¼ cup pearl (or hulled, if you'd like more bite) barley

2 cups beef broth or more to taste

canola or olive oil

1 large onion, chopped

1 pound fresh hen of the woods or king bolete mushrooms, chopped (or 2 ounces dried king boletes, rehydrated and chopped)

freshly ground pepper to taste

1 medium russet potato, shredded

2 stalks celery with leaves, chopped

2 small carrots, shredded or chopped

1 large tomato, peeled and chopped

tomato juice to taste (home canned if you have it)

2–4 large slices home-style white bread, lightly toasted

Put the shank bones and marrow bones into a large soup kettle and cover with 10 cups cold water. Bring to a rolling boil; skim off the scum. Salt heavily (my grandmother's suggestion is 3 to 4 big pinches—each one probably a scant teaspoon). Add vermouth and simmer the broth for 2 hours. Stir in the barley and continue simmering for 1 hour longer or until the meat is very tender.

Remove the meat and soup bones to a large bowl. Stir more vermouth and the beef broth into the soup and continue simmering the soup. When the bones are cool enough to handle, separate the meat and scoop the marrow from the bones (keep them separate). Cover and set aside.

Heat 1 tablespoon oil in a large skillet over medium-high heat. Add the onion; sauté for 5 minutes. Scrape into the soup broth. Add 2 tablespoons oil to skillet; sauté the mushrooms for 6 to 8 minutes or until tender. Lightly season with freshly ground pepper; remove 1 cup from the skillet and stir the rest into the soup.

Add the potato, celery, carrots, and tomato to the soup. Simmer for about 30 minutes or until the vegetables are tender. Return the meat and most of the marrow to the soup; season with salt and/or vermouth as needed. Pour in some tomato juice until, as my grandmother directs, it tastes *right*.

Mix the reserved mushrooms and marrow. Cut the toast into small pieces; top with spoonfuls of the mushroom-marrow mixture; lightly salt. Serve with big bowls of soup.

kitchen notes

This soup is an adaptation of the first supper of every visit to my grandparents when I was little. The biggest treat would be getting a small slice of home-baked bread smeared with marrow from the long-simmered beef shank and finished with a pinch of salt—as tasty as any butter.

If you know a good butcher, ask for a beef shank bone (with all the meat left on) cut into thick chunks. Then ask for a marrow bone (the shank bone without the meat) cut crosswise into slices. These will deepen the flavor of the soup broth and also give you enough marrow so everyone can have a taste.

forest mushroom & kraut-filled pierogi

makes 4 to 5 dozen (3-inch) dumplings

for the filling

1 cup (1 ounce) dried *borowik* or *grzyb prawdziwy* (king bolete) mushrooms

3 (16-ounce) jars German sauerkraut, rinsed and squeezed dry in a clean kitchen towel

2 tablespoons butter

2 medium onions, finely chopped

¾ cup finely chopped fresh king bolete mushrooms

coarse salt and freshly ground pepper to taste

for the dough

4 cups unbleached all-purpose flour plus more for kneading and rolling

1 egg

1 tablespoon olive oil

¼ teaspoon fine sea salt

about 1 cup hot water plus more if needed

for serving

melted butter, toasted bread crumbs, or crispy bacon

Place the dried mushrooms in a medium saucepan and cover with room-temperature water; cover pan and let stand overnight. Bring the mushrooms to a boil; reduce heat and simmer until they've absorbed most of the soaking liquid. Drain, cool, then finely chop. Set aside.

Spoon sauerkraut into a large saucepan. Cover with water and bring to a boil; reduce heat and simmer for several minutes. Drain and squeeze out any excess water, then finely chop and scrape into a large bowl.

Melt butter in a large skillet over medium-high heat. Sauté the onions for 6 to 8 minutes or until transparent (but not browned). Add the fresh and rehydrated mushrooms; cook and stir about 8 minutes longer. Stir in the sauerkraut and cook until everything is tender. Season with salt and pepper. Scrape back into the large bowl and let the filling cool while you make the dough.

Mound the flour on a clean surface. Make a well in the center, then drop in the egg, oil, and salt. Using a fork or your fingers, begin to mix the wet ingredients into the dry flour. Gradually add hot water as you continue mixing just until a soft dough forms. (You can begin this process in a large bowl, then turn mixture out on a flour-dusted surface.) Knead the dough for about 8 minutes or until smooth and elastic. Using half of the dough at a time, roll out on a floured surface to ⅛-inch thickness. Cut out 3-inch rounds. Place about 1 tablespoon filling in the center of each dough round; fold in half and crimp the edges together. Lay the filled pierogi out on a flour-dusted board or kitchen towels; don't stack them.

Bring a large kettle of salted water to a rapid boil. Add the pierogi with a slotted spoon, being careful not to overcrowd the top of the water as the dumplings float. Cook them for 12 to 15 minutes, then drain well. Serve immediately, drizzled with melted butter and toasted bread crumbs or crispy bacon pieces. Some cooks like to serve them with caramelized onions; John Rajtar (see next page) suggests frying leftover dumplings in butter or bacon drippings until golden brown on both sides.

(Continued next page)

kitchen notes

Pierogi—filled and boiled dumplings—are an integral part of Polish and other Slavic and Eastern European cuisines. John and Jola Rajtar (see page 2) shared their very traditional way of making wild mushroom pierogi with me, complete with photos of Jola tossing her dumpling dough into the air as she prepared it for rolling out into thin sheets. Jola cuts her pierogi rounds with a juice glass, then carefully seals the folded-over dumplings with her fingers—her own signature style of crimping. John says that every cook's crimp is unique, sort of like a fingerprint that identifies dumpling ownership. The Rajtars agree that if you're going to take the time, it's best to make a lot of dumplings all at once. You can freeze planned-overs once they're cooked.

The filling can be made a couple of days ahead and the dough can be made two hours ahead, wrapped in plastic, and refrigerated. To freeze the cooked dumplings: lay them out in a single layer on a tray and freeze, then stack in freezer containers for up to one month. Thaw before cooking.

variation

Soup Spoon Mushroom Dumplings: In the same family as pierogi are smaller mushroom-stuffed dumplings that are formed into tiny "pig's ear" shapes. A small square of dough is folded over a simple filling—rehydrated dried mushrooms, onion, and parsley—into a triangle, then the bottom corners are folded in toward each other. They can be cooked in a mushroom or chicken broth, or in Poland they're essential at Christmastime, garnishing bowls of a clear beetroot *barszcz* (the Polish equivalent of borscht). I think they're the perfect bite snuggled into a large soup spoon.

mushroom bolognese sauce

serves 6

2 cups (2 ounces) mixed dried mushrooms

1 bay leaf

2 teaspoons dried king bolete powder

4 slices thick-sliced bacon, cut crosswise in ½-inch pieces

1 large onion, chopped

2 carrots, chopped

2 stalks celery, chopped

3 cloves garlic, crushed into a paste

coarse salt and freshly ground pepper to taste

2 teaspoons finely chopped fresh marjoram

1 teaspoon finely chopped fresh thyme leaves

2 tablespoons unbleached all-purpose flour

¼ cup tomato paste

about 1½ cups beef broth

hot cooked rigatoni, if you'd like

chopped fresh parsley and red pepper flakes to taste

Place the dried mushrooms and bay leaf in a large saucepan. Cover with water; bring to a boil, then reduce heat to a simmer. Cook, stirring occasionally, for 20 to 30 minutes. Scoop out the rehydrated mushrooms; squeeze out any excess liquid and finely chop. Pour the broth through a double-folded piece of cheesecloth or a coffee filter, then return to the pan to keep warm. Stir in the mushroom powder.

Meanwhile, cook the bacon in a large deep pan over medium heat until crisp. Scoop out the bacon pieces with a slotted spoon; drain on paper toweling. Add the onion, carrots, and celery to the bacon fat. Sauté for 5 minutes; stir in the chopped mushrooms and garlic. Season with a little salt and a good grind of pepper and the herbs. Continue cooking for 10 minutes.

Sprinkle the flour over the vegetables and stir to blend it in. Add the tomato paste, then the warm mushroom broth combined with enough beef broth to equal 3 cups. Cook and stir over medium heat until the sauce is slightly thickened.

Serve the sauce over pasta, sprinkled with crumbled bacon, parsley, and red pepper flakes.

kitchen notes

Add some chopped fresh autumn mushrooms if there are still some about. Michael says he's actually found black trumpets flourishing until the first snow.

braised rabbit in a mushroomy rosemary dijon sauce

serves 4

1 (2½– to 3-pound) rabbit, cut into pieces

⅓ cup classic Dijon mustard

coarse salt and freshly ground pepper to taste

3 tablespoons olive oil

3 tablespoons butter, divided

2 cups dry white wine

1 large sprig fresh rosemary

2 medium shallots, finely chopped

2 cups Freezer Wild Mushroom Duxelles (see page 284), thawed

1 cup crème fraîche or heavy cream

1 tablespoon whole-grain Dijon mustard

1 tablespoon chopped fresh flat-leaf parsley

Brush one side of the rabbit pieces with some Dijon; season with salt and pepper. Heat the oil and 1 tablespoon butter in a large deep skillet or two-handled braiser pan or enameled casserole over medium-high heat. Brown the rabbit in batches, mustard-side down, for about 10 minutes or until golden, removing the pieces to a tray. Turn the pieces over, brush with more mustard, season with salt and pepper, and brown on the other side.

With all the browned rabbit pieces on the tray, pour the wine into the pan. Scrape up all the browned bits from the bottom of the pan. Return the rabbit to the pan; tuck in the rosemary sprig, cover, and simmer for about 40 minutes or until the rabbit is tender.

Meanwhile, melt the remaining 2 tablespoons butter in a medium skillet over medium-high heat. Sauté the shallots for about 3 minutes; add the mushroom duxelles. Cook and stir for about 4 minutes or until everything is tender. Set aside.

When the rabbit is done, transfer the pieces to a serving platter (discard the rosemary sprig); lightly tent with foil. Bring the cooking juices to a boil; cook for 5 to 10 minutes or until reduced by half. Stir in the crème fraîche, whole-grain mustard, and the mushroom mixture. Simmer for 5 to 10 minutes; season with salt and pepper. Pour the sauce over the rabbit and sprinkle with the parsley.

kitchen notes

This stew (*en cocotte*) to me is the essence of the French winter kitchen. I couldn't wait to find a rabbit at the farmers' market when I returned from Paris years ago so I could make this country bistro standard. You may have wild rabbit in your freezer, but if not you can order one from a good butcher. My longtime favorite Dijon mustard is Maille, which is quite spicy without being too incendiary and is available both smoothly ground and in a more rustic style, filled with whole mustard seed.

a winter tonic

serves 4

4 large room-temperature eggs

2 tablespoons toasted sesame oil

1 cup finely chopped red onion

¼ cup white miso paste

1 (1-inch) piece fresh gingerroot, peeled and grated

3 cloves garlic, finely chopped

4 cups water

4 cups good-quality unsalted chicken stock

1 cup (1 ounce) mixed dried mushrooms (king bolete, morel, lobster)

½ cup uncooked buckwheat groats (kasha), rinsed and drained

2 baby carrots with tops, trimmed and sliced

¾ pound baby bok choy or napa cabbage, sliced crosswise

2 green onions, sliced

2 tablespoons rice vinegar

Place eggs in a small saucepan; cover with water. Bring to a steady simmer; cook for 7 minutes. Transfer eggs to a bowl of ice water. Cool and peel; set aside.

Heat the oil in a large saucepan over medium-high heat. Sauté the red onion, miso, and ginger for about 10 minutes or until the mixture starts to brown. Stir in the garlic; sauté for 1 minute.

Add the water, stock, and mushrooms. Simmer for 10 minutes. Stir in the buckwheat and carrot; simmer for 15 minutes or until tender. Add the bok choy and green onions; continue to cook for 5 minutes. Stir in the vinegar and ladle the soup into bowls. Cut each egg in half lengthwise and place 2 halves in each bowl.

kitchen notes

A steaming bowl of broth filled with restorative ingredients—and that might even clear a stuffed head—is always welcome in the dead of winter. This chicken-miso broth is enriched with some off-the-shelf dried mushrooms, simple vegetables, and fragrant ginger. Buckwheat groats are actually a seed rather than a grain and are the principal ingredient in Japanese soba noodles, but also are toasted and made into fluffy pilafs or tossed with pasta in Eastern European cuisines.

The Larder

Preserving Your Mushrooms for the Future

You can eat just so many mushrooms in the first days after a good harvest, so longtime hunters choose among a handful of ways to transform their overflow into pantry staples. Each species is best preserved by methods that will maintain its unique flavor.

Drying: For Intensely Concentrated, Bold Flavor

Dried mushrooms and mushroom powder have a long shelf life and are space saving, versatile pantry ingredients that add earthy richness to a wide variety of recipes. Because the flavor is concentrated you don't need as much in a recipe.

The best species for drying (in our collection) are morels, lobsters, king boletes, and black trumpets. All maintain their deep flavor and rehydrate beautifully. Michael has a stunning collection of tiny dried morels and other gorgeous sliced mushrooms that become the heart of his in-the-moment recipes (see page 282 for his Elegant Pantry Porcini Cream Soup). Other mushrooms—like giant puffballs, hedgehogs, and hen of the woods—make flavorful powders. They are worth the drying time and are easily buzzed up in a spice grinder.

You can air-dry, oven-dry, or use a stacked-tray dehydrator to make short work of a nice basket of mushrooms. But if you're serious about using drying as a preservation method, acquire a workhorse dehydrator that has a good fan system; I like having a top-mounted fan so any juices from food won't drip down into it. There are lots of styles to choose from, but having even heat flow and the ability to adjust the temperature are the most important features.

For even drying, keep all the mushrooms around the same thickness: if you want to dry a batch of tiny morels, don't mix them with trays of other mushrooms that are sliced (you can remove trays as the mushrooms finish drying, but it takes more oversight). For most of the mushrooms, brush them off or lightly rinse, then slice them thinly and distribute them evenly, and not touching, on the trays. Keep the temperature setting below 140 degrees (the lower the temperature, the longer it takes) and dry the mushrooms until they're brittle—any residual moisture increases the chance they'll mold once you store them in closed containers. I dehydrated a large batch of sliced lobster mushrooms at close to 120 degrees and it took about seven hours for them to be completely dry. Black trumpets (one of the nicest to dry, as they maintain a woodsy, slightly sweet flavor) took only about four hours. Allow the mushrooms to cool completely before filling up covered jars or sealed bags.

Plumping Them Up

To rehydrate any of the mushrooms, you can choose a number of ways depending on how you want to use them. A slower, cooler soak will keep more of the flavor inside the mushrooms; using very hot water or rehydrating in broth will release more of the mushroomy flavor, but the liquid can be cooked back into the mushrooms in a hot skillet or be used to make stock or soups. Because there's usually some dirt or sand trapped with the mushrooms despite best efforts to clean them before drying, straining the soaking liquid through cheesecloth in a colander or a paper coffee filter works well. If you think the plumped mushrooms are still a bit gritty, it's okay to give them a quick rinse before chopping them or adding them to a hot pan. The technique of using water to continually deglaze a pan as foods slowly brown is a perfect way to use the flavorful soaking liquid, and, when sautéing the rehydrated mushrooms or other vegetables or aromatics, it's a distinctive way of steaming and concentrating flavors. Lastly, you can cover the mushrooms with water in a saucepan, then bring to a boil. Reduce the heat and simmer the mushrooms until they're very tender and all the water has been absorbed or evaporated.

Mushroom Powders

Dried mushrooms can be easily pulverized in an electric spice mill or coffee grinder, creating sophisticated seasoning powders (add any salvaged crumbles left from drying mushrooms or ones that get crushed during storage). King boletes, lobsters, giant puffballs, hedgehogs, even black trumpets can be stirred into sauces, soups, or stews, enriching and intensifying their flavor. Mix with salt and spices for instant dry grill rubs for meat and poultry. Or dredge mild fish fillets or chicken breasts in a mushroom powder tossed with crisp crumbs for pan- or oven-roasting. But remember that these powders are intensely flavored, so experiment with how much you use.

Elegant Pantry Porcini Cream Soup with Roquefort Cream & Chives: Cover 4 cups sliced dried king boletes (porcini) with water in a large saucepan. Bring to a boil; reduce heat and simmer until the mushrooms are tender. Add 3 cups chicken stock, ½ cup dry white wine, 1 large peeled and chopped russet potato, 1 bay leaf, and coarse salt and freshly ground pepper to taste. Simmer for 20 minutes or until the potato is very tender. Meanwhile, chop 1 medium white onion; sauté in olive oil until tender; stir into soup. Carefully pour the soup into a large food processor bowl fit with the metal blade. Process the soup until smooth and thick—thin with a little more stock if you'd like. Return the soup to the saucepan; stir in 2 cups heavy cream. Whisk some sour cream and crumbled Roquefort (or a good local blue) cheese together until smooth. Serve the soup in small bowls, with a swirl of the blue cheese sauce and a generous sprinkle of sliced fresh chives.

Freezing: Taking a Page from the French

Some species, like chanterelles, lion's mane, and chicken of the woods, are more delicious preserved in a classic sauté—or more specifically as a *duxelles* mixture. It's a French cook's easiest way to concentrate the meaty savoriness of mushrooms. Morels and black trumpets are good candidates for this technique. When the mushrooms are very finely chopped and cooked, then frozen, they impart their natural flavors once thawed and added to recipes—and I like the almost sausage-like texture. A simple lasagna built with classic ingredients becomes something distinctly wonderful with layers of mushroom duxelles. Using a combination of mushrooms is easier, too, if you have them ready and waiting in the freezer. Morels or king boletes offer a distinctive high note, some black trumpets add a balancing sweetness, and hedgehogs or hen of the woods provides a nice base note to lasagna or a creamy risotto.

The key here is removing the water that will become ice crystals when you freeze the mushrooms—ice that will break down their texture. Begin by finely chopping the mushrooms; the classic technique results in the cooked mushrooms developing an almost paste-like (or pâté) texture: you can choose to slice or more coarsely chop them. Start with a dry sauté in a large hot skillet (be sure the mushrooms aren't crowded in the pan or they'll steam rather than brown) or slick the pan with a little fat first. Then the goal is to drive off moisture in the mushrooms; continue to cook them until they're tender, then add a little more fat and/or seasonings if you'd like. Scrape them into freezer containers. Or do as Michael does and vacuum-seal them for longer freezer storage.

freezer wild mushroom duxelles

makes about 2 cups

1 pound fresh wild mushrooms (morels, pheasant backs, chanterelles, black trumpets, hedgehogs, chicken of the woods)

3 tablespoons unsalted butter or olive oil, divided

⅓ cup finely chopped shallots

coarse salt and freshly ground pepper to taste

½ teaspoon dried thyme, if you'd like

¼ cup dry white wine, vermouth, or dry sherry, if you'd like

Finely chop the mushrooms in a food processor. Heat 1 tablespoon of the butter or oil in a large skillet over medium-high heat. Add the mushrooms and shallots; sprinkle lightly with salt, a quick grind of pepper, and thyme.

Cook, stirring frequently, for 6 to 8 minutes or until the mushrooms release their juices. Continue cooking until the mushrooms are dry and begin to brown. Stir in the remaining butter or oil, then pour in the wine. Cook, stirring frequently, until the wine has evaporated. Cool.

Spoon into freezer bags (use a vacuum-sealer for the best results and longest shelf life in the freezer) or small containers. Freeze for up to 6 months.

kitchen notes

This very basic template is a classic way to transform mushrooms into the foundation for remarkable recipes—and is one of the best ways to preserve a fresh harvest in the freezer. Michael likes to dry sauté the mushrooms to start, until they release their juices. Then he swirls in some butter or oil, white wine, salt, and pepper. Once the mixture is tender and all the liquid is evaporated, he cools it, then vacuum-seals it in bags. He carefully notes with a freezer marker what species they are, the volume, and the date. If you have fewer mushrooms, simply reduce the proportions.

• • • • •

Pickling: An Exercise in Flavor Bending

Like so many foodstuffs that needed to be stored away for a cold winter's night, some long-ago (and very astute) hunter figured out how to salt meats to add to his larder for the winter, while gatherers, and eventually farmers and gardeners, figured out how to preserve plants (and fungi) by using both salt and acidic liquids. Pickling mushrooms is part of this global culinary art. Not only an ancient preservation technique, it alters the taste and texture of mushrooms in extraordinary ways, from zesty and herbal to spicy-sour or sweet-tart with an appealingly tender bite.

In our collection of wild fungi, I think golden chanterelles make some of the most enchanting pickles, especially the nearly perfect Lilliputian buttons. Hen of the woods and king boletes are lovely as well. Oyster mushrooms, simmered in a pickling brine made with more delicate rice vinegar, are simple and elegant. I'm a big fan of quick pickles (see page 299 for Pickled Hen of the Woods), but that means making smaller batches that can be stored in the fridge and eaten quickly. If you're in it for the long haul, be prepared to do a little sterilizing—but it's always worth the time. I follow my grandmother's method of heating up the brine—which is perfect for cooking the mushrooms—then filling the jars. No cumbersome canning kettle needed.

· · · · ·

a basic american-style pickled mushroom

makes about 2½ quarts

brine

3 cups white distilled or rice vinegar

1 cup white wine (dry or lightly sweet)

1 cup water

¼ cup sugar

2 tablespoons pickling salt

½ teaspoon black peppercorns

3 cloves garlic, sliced

2 bay leaves, broken

pickling spices, dill seeds, or fresh herbs to taste

mushrooms

3 pounds fresh wild mushrooms, torn, halved, or quartered—depending on size

Combine brine ingredients and bring to a boil, then add the mushrooms. Reduce heat and simmer for about 10 minutes. Fill sterilized canning jars with the mushrooms and pour in the hot brine. Screw on sterilized lids and let cool. You'll hear the "ping" as the jars seal. When you serve these, drizzle with a flavorful oil and serve with grilled flatbreads or as part of an appetizer spread.

woodland finishing salt

makes about 1½ cups

½ cup very coarse sea salt crystals

⅓ cup small broken pieces of very dry king bolete or chanterelle mushrooms

2 tablespoons Tellicherry peppercorns

1 tablespoon pink peppercorns

1 tablespoon grains of paradise, if you'd like

2 teaspoons coriander seed

2 teaspoons roasted dried garlic chunks

Mix all the ingredients in a large mortar and pestle or spice grinder. Simply crush or lightly buzz up the mixture, depending on how you'd like to use it. Store in an airtight jar in a cool, dark place for up to a year (if it lasts that long).

kitchen notes

The first time I tasted a similar seasoning salt I was impressed by the intense savoriness the dried mushrooms gave to what could be a special grilling salt or inspiration for winter roasted foods. Search for some grains of paradise to round out the overall flavor. The glossy brown seeds from a plant in West Africa (that is related to ginger and cardamom) were once upon a time a cheaper alternative to black peppercorns, offering a light floral, spice-laced taste with a long, slow burn on the tongue. They're hard to find now (order them online from a good spice vendor), but I think they're worth trying. Their zestiness complements other spices like coriander, and I love them ground with peppercorns and as a unique pick-me-up in pickling spice blends. The moniker "paradise" was pure marketing, bestowed by long-ago spice traders trying to convince buyers the seeds were harvested in Eden.

For everyday use, pour the salt and spice mixture into a glass spice bottle with a grinder top (find one with a ceramic grinder blade or recycle a grinder bottle from a purchased blend if the cap screws off). Play around with other seasoning combinations, like aromatic black trumpets ground with a traditional lavender-spiked *herbs de Provence* or king boletes blended with rosemary, thyme, oregano, basil, and fennel seed—with maybe a few broken dried chiles thrown in to perk things up.

porcini-rosemary crumb coating

makes 2¾ cups

3 tablespoons fresh rosemary leaves

olive oil

½ cup (½ ounce) dried king bolete (porcini) mushrooms

2 cups panko bread crumbs

coarse salt and freshly ground pepper to taste

Mix the rosemary leaves with a few drops of oil. Spread them out in a glass pie plate. Microwave on high power for about 2½ minutes or until leaves look dry. Cool.

Grind the dry rosemary and dried mushrooms in batches in a spice mill or clean coffee grinder until powdered. Mix the bread crumbs with the rosemary-mushroom powder, salt, and pepper. Store in an airtight container or glass jar.

kitchen notes
Use this mixture to coat fish, chicken, or pork before baking or frying. Dip fish fillets, chicken pieces, or pork cutlets in some beaten egg before dredging in the crumb coating, then drizzle with a little olive oil if baking.

· · · · ·

mushroom-espresso rub

makes about ⅔ cup

¼ cup (¼ ounce) dried king bolete, chanterelle, or lobster mushrooms, broken into pieces

3 tablespoons dark roasted espresso beans

1 tablespoon roasted garlic granules

2 teaspoons black peppercorns or grains of paradise

2 tablespoons coarse salt

1 tablespoon dark brown sugar

1 tablespoon smoked paprika

In a spice mill or clean coffee grinder pulverize in turn the mushrooms, espresso beans, garlic, and peppercorns. Add each to a bowl and stir in the salt, brown sugar, and paprika. Store in an airtight container or glass jar.

kitchen notes
This fragrant spice blend is great rubbed on steaks or poultry pieces. If you'd like a more garlicky edge, skip the dried garlic and rub a mixture of crushed fresh garlic and olive oil over the meat before pressing on the mushroom-coffee mixture.

compound wild mushroom herb butter

makes about 1 pound

3 tablespoons extra-virgin olive oil

1 clove garlic or 1 small shallot, finely chopped

1 cup finely chopped fresh wild mushrooms (pheasant back, chanterelle, king bolete, or hen of the woods)

1½ cups (¾ pound) fresh dairy butter, softened

2 tablespoons finely chopped fresh herbs (chives, thyme, sage, rosemary)

freshly ground pepper to taste

Heat oil in a heavy skillet over medium heat. Add garlic or shallot; cook and stir for a few minutes until fragrant. Add the mushrooms; cook and stir frequently until they release their juices and begin to brown. Scrape into a medium bowl and allow to cool to room temperature.

Add the butter and herbs to the bowl with the mushrooms. With a wooden spoon or rubber spatula mix everything together until well blended, seasoning with a few good grinds of pepper as you like.

Spoon the butter mixture onto a piece of waxed paper or plastic wrap; roll up and form into a tight log (or two). Refrigerate until very firm. Store in the fridge for up to a month or in the freezer for 6 months.

kitchen notes

Any butter enhanced with mushrooms and herbs will keep for one to two months in the fridge or can be frozen for several months. Butter and other fats are natural preservatives, so make the most of keeping a pretty butter log on hand for as long as mushroom season lasts. Plop a pat on a sizzling steak, slather on steamed corn, spread on a warm slice of toasted country bread, or bump up the savoriness of braised greens. And if you've nearly been skunked on a hunt, use your slender harvest—no matter what the variety—to make a batch of this earthy butter.

elegant black trumpet-shallot butter

makes about ¾ cup

½ cup (½ ounce) dried black trumpet mushrooms

1 teaspoon olive oil

3 tablespoons very finely chopped shallot

½ cup (4 ounces) fresh dairy butter, softened

a few shakes Worcestershire sauce or to taste

lemon juice and freshly ground pepper to taste

Cover the mushrooms with warm tap water; let stand for about 20 minutes or until plumped and softened. Swish the mushrooms around and lift from the soaking liquid, leaving any grit in the bowl. Squeeze any excess liquid from the mushrooms, then chop very finely. Strain the liquid through a double-folded piece of cheesecloth or a coffee filter.

Heat the oil in a medium skillet over medium-high heat. Add the chopped mushrooms and shallot; sauté for 2 minutes. Pour the filtered soaking liquid into the skillet; simmer until evaporated and the mushrooms and shallots are very tender. Cool.

Stir the mushroom-shallot mixture into the softened butter; season with Worcestershire, a splash of lemon, and ground pepper. Mix until well blended; spoon onto a piece of waxed paper or plastic wrap and form the butter into a log. Chill until firm. Keep chilled or freeze up to 6 months.

kitchen notes

The little black dress of compound butters: visually arresting, with a slightly fruity savoriness. Make other compound butters with dried morels or king boletes, rehydrating part of them and pulverizing the rest into a powder to stir into the butter.

roasted wild mushroom stock

makes 2½ quarts

2 large yellow onions, unpeeled, cut into wedges

1 medium carrot, scrubbed but not peeled, coarsely chopped

5 cloves unpeeled garlic

1–2 cups of any vegetable scraps you might have (potato or carrot peels and tops or asparagus ends)—this is up to you, but it's nice to round out the flavor

1 pound fresh wild mushrooms (chanterelles, oysters, lobsters, hen of the woods, king boletes), coarsely chopped

2 tablespoons olive oil

½ cup (½ ounce) mixed dried wild mushrooms, quickly rinsed

1 bunch flat-leaf Italian parsley

6 sprigs fresh thyme

1½ teaspoons black peppercorns

1 bay leaf

10 cups water

Heat oven to 425 degrees. Spread the onions, carrot, garlic, vegetables scraps, and fresh mushrooms out on a large parchment-lined rimmed baking sheet. Drizzle with oil and roast, stirring occasionally, for 30 to 40 minutes.

Scrape the roasted vegetables into a large stockpot with the dried mushrooms, parsley, thyme, peppercorns, and bay leaf. Pour in the water; bring to a boil.

Reduce heat and simmer, partially covered, for 1 to 1½ hours or until the stock has a very defined mushroomy flavor. Pour the stock through several layers of cheesecloth or a large fine-mesh strainer into a large bowl. Press all the liquid from the solids, then discard (or compost) them. Let the stock cool, then pour into ice cube trays, freezer containers, or jars. Chill the stock for up to 3 days or freeze for up to 6 months.

kitchen notes

It's quite confusing, from the grocery aisle to cookbooks, when the words *broth* and *stock* are used interchangeably. Both should be made from long-simmered ingredients, sometimes browned on the stovetop or in the oven beforehand. But a broth is seasoned with salt, while a stock should have no salt, and often few other seasonings, added. A simple stock is the better choice when you want total control of the level of seasonings in a dish, like for a sauce. But a well-seasoned broth that is already flavor balanced with salt will meld well with soups and stews—dishes that can be salt-challenged from the start and benefit from the savory liquid.

Vegetarian Mushroom Dashi: To make an Asian-flavored broth for noodle soups, simmer some dried kombu (kelp) in the mushroom stock. Add 2 (4-inch) pieces of kombu that have been gently wiped with a damp paper towel to 6 cups mushroom stock. Bring the broth to just under a boil; simmer for a few seconds, then remove the kombu (you can chop it up to add to a soup or compost it).

smoky maple lobster bacon

makes about 1 cup

½ pound fresh lobster
mushrooms, cleaned and thinly
sliced (about ⅛ inch thick)

olive oil

smoked salt and freshly ground
pepper to taste

1 tablespoon maple syrup

1 teaspoon smoked paprika

Heat oven to 350 degrees. Line 2 large rimmed baking sheets with parchment. Lay mushroom slices out on baking sheets in a single layer; brush with oil. Turn them over and lightly brush with a little more oil. Sprinkle with smoked salt and pepper. Bake the mushrooms for 20 minutes. Turn them over and bake for 20 minutes longer.

Mix the maple syrup and paprika. Brush onto the mushrooms. Continue baking for about 15 minutes or until the mushrooms are bubbling and crisp around the edges.

Allow the mushrooms to cool completely. Store in an airtight container at room temperature for no longer than a week.

kitchen notes

These mushroom chips are still slightly chewy and are smoky-sweet, making them a surprisingly satisfying meatless substitute for bacon. Sprinkle the pieces into a warm spinach or German potato salad, over roasted vegetables, or onto grilled cheesy flatbreads. If you don't have a cache of lobsters, slice up some king boletes or chicken of the woods.

pantry mushroom-onion jam

makes about 4 cups

2 cups (about 2 ounces) mixed dried mushrooms

2 tablespoons butter

3 large onions, thinly sliced

1 large shallot, sliced

coarse salt and freshly ground pepper to taste

3 tablespoons brown sugar

2 tablespoons red wine vinegar

2 teaspoons chopped fresh thyme leaves

¼ cup sliced fresh garlic chives, if you'd like

Pour 2 cups warm tap water over the mushrooms in a medium bowl; let them soak 20 to 30 minutes or until they're plumped and softened. Scoop them out with a slotted spoon and squeeze any excess water back into the soaking liquid. Coarsely chop the mushrooms; set aside. Strain the liquid through double-folded cheesecloth or a coffee filter; set aside.

Meanwhile, melt the butter in a large heavy skillet over medium heat. Add the onions and shallots; season with salt and pepper. Cover and cook, stirring frequently, for about 20 minutes or until the mixture starts to caramelize.

Stir in the mushrooms. Cook and stir for 5 to 10 minutes or until the vegetables are very tender and browned. Add the mushroom soaking liquid, brown sugar, vinegar, and thyme; cook for about 10 minutes or until the liquid reduces by half. Stir in the chives.

Spoon into jars or freezer containers. Refrigerate for up to a week or freeze for up to 6 months.

kitchen notes

Savory mixtures of slow-cooked aromatics like onions, shallots, or leeks are even more luscious with an injection of rehydrated wild mushrooms. Usually served as a condiment for roasted meats, these jams, conserves, or marmalades (which rarely have any citrus involved) are given a sweet-tart or sour edge, offering a subtle or bold flavor contrast to whatever they accompany.

toasted mushroom–chile dipping oil

makes 1 cup

1 cup (1 ounce) dried
king bolete, lobster, and/or
black trumpet mushrooms

1 fresh serrano chile, finely
chopped, or 2–3 small dried
hot chiles (use what you like)

1 cup extra-virgin olive oil

Break the mushrooms into smaller pieces with your hands; lightly toast in a dry skillet over medium heat until fragrant. Cool, then transfer the pieces to a spice or clean coffee grinder and pulverize until finely ground.

Mix the mushroom powder and chiles with the oil in a medium saucepan; place over medium-low heat. Cook, keeping the heat at a low simmer, for about 4 minutes or until oil reaches 180 degrees on an instant-read thermometer. Cool, then strain through a triple-folded piece of cheesecloth in a colander set over a bowl.

Decant the oil into a clean bottle or jar and seal well. Refrigerate for up to 3 weeks. Oil will become cloudy and solidified when chilled; allow it to come to room temperature when you want to use it.

kitchen notes
This fragrantly earthy oil is the real deal compared to oils that are enhanced artificially with mushroom flavoring. It's easy to make, so simmer up just enough to use quickly, before the delicate aroma and flavor fade. If you pour the oil into a bottle, for a pretty appearance you can hydrate some sliced dry mushrooms, squeeze them very dry, and include them as you're infusing the oil. I like this oil drizzled over roasted vegetables or mixed with herbs for dipping crusty bread.

pickled hen of the woods

makes 2 pints

for the mushrooms

1 pound fresh hen of the woods mushrooms, torn or cut into bite-size pieces

8 large cloves garlic, sliced lengthwise

olive oil

coarse salt

for the pickling brine

½ cup white wine or rice vinegar

1 tablespoon brown sugar

1 tablespoon finely chopped flat-leaf parsley

2 teaspoons grated lemon zest

1 teaspoon coriander seed

½ teaspoon fennel seed

¼ teaspoon crushed red pepper

Heat oven to 425 degrees. Line a rimmed baking sheet with parchment paper. Spread the mushrooms and garlic out on baking sheet; drizzle with 1 tablespoon oil and season with 1 teaspoon salt. Roast for 20 to 25 minutes or until the mushrooms and garlic are tender.

Meanwhile, pour the vinegar into a medium bowl. Stir in the brown sugar, parsley, lemon zest, coriander, fennel, and red pepper. Stir in the warm mushrooms and garlic; season with 1 teaspoon salt and drizzle with 1 tablespoon oil. Cover and refrigerate until chilled. Spoon into jars; refrigerate for up to 1 month.

kitchen notes

Serve pickled mushrooms as part of a tapas tray or with chilled oysters and a smoky Scotch.

wild mushroom–wine simmer sauce

makes 3½ cups

4 tablespoons butter, divided

1½ pounds mixed fresh wild mushrooms, finely chopped

1 large leek, rinsed well and sliced lengthwise and then crosswise into thin slices

coarse salt and freshly ground pepper to taste

1¼ cups dry white or red wine

2 teaspoons dried wild mushroom powder

1 tablespoon cornstarch dissolved in 2 tablespoons water

1–2 tablespoons chopped fresh herbs (flat-leaf parsley, marjoram, thyme, rosemary, or sage)

Melt 2 tablespoons butter in a large heavy skillet over medium-high heat. Add the mushrooms and leek; cook, stirring frequently, for about 8 minutes or until the mushrooms release their juices and begin to brown. Stir in the remaining 2 tablespoons butter; season with salt and pepper.

Stir in the wine and mushroom powder. Bring to a simmer; cook for about 2 minutes, then stir in the cornstarch slurry. Cook and stir until the sauce thickens. Stir in the herbs. Cool; spoon into jars or vacuum-seal in freezer bags. Refrigerate for up to a week or freeze for up to 6 months.

kitchen notes

Simmer sauces are really high-quality cooking shortcuts, taking away the burden of making your own last-minute or long-simmered sauces. I see them as strategic meal starters, and one more uncomplicated way to preserve a fresh mushroom harvest. Because mushrooms bring a richness to any dish, a simmer sauce can be the heavy flavor workhorse for a quick pasta supper, a saucy skillet of sautéed chicken, or a side sauce for baked fish or grilled steaks.

Acknowledgments

First and foremost, I thank my wife, Heather. Her patience with the loss of her dining room table for the better part of two years while I set up shop to write this book and the calm with which she managed our lives around this project made this task infinitely easier. From her good-hearted willingness to move a bowl of "past prime" mushrooms from the fridge to the back patio and the cheerful manner with which she informed me of such science experiments to her acceptance of the postponement of many other plans was immeasurably supportive and the heart of my success in completing this book.

Thank you to my parents, who instilled in me an affinity and reverence for the outdoors, especially to my mother, who introduced me to the kitchen, forging a love for foods both cultivated and found.

Thank you to Todd Overland and Ryan Schoen for the countless hours spent in the woods and all the laughs that made this endeavor far richer. Without your scouting, camaraderie, companionship, and generosity, this work would have been impossible.

Thank you to Chef Alan Bergo of foragerchef.com for your constant inspiration and friendship.

Thank you to Anna Gerenday for your generous wisdom and hardy spirit. Your passion for and knowledge of the fungal world is an inspiration and font of infinite motivation for my mycological exploration.

And finally, a deep and resounding thank-you to family and friends who fill my email and text streams with photo inquiries of mysterious mushrooms that have kept me distracted and intrigued at all the right times throughout this process.

Michael Karns

My utmost gratitude to Kandace, my best friend and wife of nearly thirty years, who has been supportive and patient with my unending creative endeavors, holding down the home front and managing the photo studio business.

Thank you to Lisa Golden Schroeder for all the years of great food styling, writing, and a willingness to collaborate and execute professional and personal work just for the love of it. I always can count on you for a last-minute brainstorming session. You are a professional and true friend.

Thank you to Michael Karns for the insight into mushroom foraging, an activity I will continue for a lifetime. The time Michael dedicated to finding every mushroom featured in this book was greatly appreciated. Oh, and thanks for removing a wasp stinger in my rear side after we encountered that ground nest.

I also thank longtime friend and colleague David Spohn for agreeing to design and illustrate this project for us. Dave's countless years of experience in book design and illustration combined with his passion and interest in the outdoors made him the perfect fit for this book.

Thanks to Maizee, my retired bird dog who now likes to go mushroom hunting with her master.

Last and most I thank my mom, Ilene Becker, for raising me in a creative environment. As an artist she taught me how to see.

Dennis Becker

First and foremost, I need to express my deep appreciation for the creative relationship I've had with Dennis Becker, collaborating in new ways weekly, for more years than we care to admit. His eye for and love of good food makes me a much better cook and stylist. And to Michael Karns, whose exhaustive knowledge of the natural world and precision in everything he does pushes me to reexamine how I share ideas in the kitchen. This book wouldn't exist without his expertise—along with his treasure trove of a freezer and pantry filled with little bags of frozen duxelles and jars of exquisitely dried morels. And never-ending thanks to Kandace Becker for her patience as her husband disappeared for evening and weekend photo shoots—and for wiping down the always slightly grimy studio kitchen.

I can never say how much my mother, Ferol Smith Golden, is my culinary inspiration. Now in her mid-eighties, she's still an adventurer in the kitchen, regularly suggesting yet one more way to eat a mushroom. I hear her in my ear, both figuratively and for real, every day. And to my wonderful husband, Mark Schroeder, who is always my biggest booster and with whom I've explored the wilderness and walked in the woods for over thirty years.

My list of friends and believers who shared glimpses into their very personal memories and recipes is long—loving family snapshots. But I can't say how much I value my friendship and counsel from Betsy Robinson, Pegi Lee, Bea Krinke, Susan Moores, and Marcela Sorondo—longtime colleagues, each opening a door to deep wellsprings of food knowledge and connections. Hmong chef Yia Vang, Polish stylist and artist John Rajtar, and avid mushroom hunter and photographer Brittany Johnson and her dad, Dennis Gadbois, all provided enlightening insights and recipes and hunted down mushrooms we needed for recipe testing and photography. To Brian and Sue Mielke—for not only the gorgeous pottery we've featured in many of our recipe photos but for allowing me to harvest part of their front yard hen of the woods and for leading me to hidden neighborhood fruitings of pheasant backs and flourishes of wild edible greens. And to Julie Kean, basket weaver extraordinaire in the north woods of Minnesota, and her chanterelle-hunting daughter, Meadow Adams—thank you for letting a complete stranger ask a lot of questions and place custom basket orders from afar. You all made this project possible and so much richer.

In memoriam, I'd like to recognize my grandmothers Janice Wills Smith and Barbara McIntyre Wills and great-aunt Janet Bradley, who passed on their love of cooking and who inspired some of these recipes. Ray Schroeder, my father-in-law, and his German grandmother Ida, who were passionate mushroom hunters and the source of some very entertaining family lore about woodland adventures (including a run-in with the wrong mushrooms, complete with a trip to the emergency room). And Sandy Bloom, one of my mother's closest friends, who always believed in me as a cook and was sharing mushroom recipes up to just a few months before she died.

And finally, we're so grateful to our editor Shannon Pennefeather, whose encouragement and relaxed style kept panic at bay. And to Ann Burckhardt, whose stellar career as a food writer, cookbook author, and culinary historian in the Twin Cities is unparalleled—it's such an honor that she's played the essential role of indexer for us. She set me on the road to book publishing many years ago, recommending me for my first book project, and then suggesting we share the 2fish1dish blog post about stalking wild mushrooms with the Minnesota Historical Society Press.

Lisa Golden Schroeder

Recipe Index

Subject Index

Michael Karns, Lisa Golden Schroeder, and Dennis Becker

Michael Karns began foraging as a teenager in north-central Arkansas. His passion for great food and a slightly obsessive compulsion for learning have led him to delve deeply into mycology and the delicious treasures the forest has to offer. Michael is a certified mycological identification expert in the area of food service and sourcing, a member of the North American Mycological Association (NAMA) and the Minnesota Mycological Society (MMS), and owner/proprietor of "Found Foods" (foundfoods.com)—a purveyor of wild-sourced and artisan-created edibles.

Dennis Becker is a commercial photographer specializing in food photography. His work for local and international food companies can be seen in cookbooks and magazines and on billboards, food packaging, websites, and social media. Evidence of his extensive experience with advertising agencies across the nation can be seen at dennisbeckerphotography.com. Photographing *Untamed Mushrooms* inspired and taught him about the varieties of mushrooms that are truly works of art—and good to eat. Dennis works out of his studio in the Minneapolis area.

Lisa Golden Schroeder is a veteran food writer, food stylist for commercial photography, and entrepreneur. A degree in nutrition and journalism along with a stint at École de Cuisine La Varenne informed her work as a corporate test kitchen professional and cookbook editor. Foodesigns.com features her food styling portfolio and *trifling with food*, an eclectic kitchen journal. Her second home is on the edge of the northeastern Minnesota wilderness, where identifying wild foods along forest trails is a constant source of fascination.